CHEAT CODE

C☻DE

EXPLOSION

⬧ DANGER ⬧ **FOR HANDHELDS** ⬧ COMBUSTIBLE ⬧

FLIP THIS BOOK OVER FOR HOME CONSOLES PlayStation® 3 Nintendo Wii™ Xbox 360™ PlayStation® 2	**LOOK FOR CODEY** *When you see Codey's face, you've found the newest and coolest codes!*

CHEAT CODE EXPLOSION

EXCLUSIVE SCHOLASTIC EDITION

© 2008 DK/BradyGAMES, a division of Penguin Group (USA) Inc. BradyGAMES® is a registered trademark of Penguin Group (USA) Inc. All rights reserved, including the right of reproduction in whole or in part in any form.

DK/BradyGames, a division of Penguin Group (USA) Inc.
800 East 96th Street, 3rd Floor
Indianapolis, IN 46240

ISBN: 978-0-7440-1075-6

Printing Code: The rightmost double-digit number is the year of the book's printing; the rightmost single-digit number is the number of the book's printing. For example, 08-1 shows that the first printing of the book occurred in 2008.

11 10 09 08   4 3 2 1

Printed in the USA.

CREDITS

Title Manager
Tim Fitzpatrick

Cheat Code and Screenshot Editor
Michael Owen

Book Designer
Doug Wilkins

Production Designer
Wil Cruz

BRADYGAMES STAFF

Publisher
David Waybright

Editor-In-Chief
H. Leigh Davis

Licensing Director
Mike Degler

Marketing Director
Debby Neubauer

International Translations
Brian Saliba

NINTENDO DS™

TABLE OF CONTENTS

ADVANCE WARS: DAYS OF RUIN

UNLOCK COS

Complete the following missions to unlock the corresponding CO.

COMPLETE MISSION	CO UNLOCKED
12	Tasha
13	Gage
14	Forthsythe
20	Waylon
21	Greyfield
24	Penny
25	Tabitha
26	Caulder

ADVANCE WARS: DUAL STRIKE

ADVANCE WARS MAP

Select Map from the Design Room menu and immediately press and hold L + R. You will get a map that spells out Advance Wars. By having old versions of advance wars inserted in your DS at the same time as Dual Strike, you can unlock new buyables at the the Battle Maps Shop!

ADVANCE WARPAPER

Insert Advance Wars in the GBA slot of your Nintendo DS. Start Advance Wars: Dual Strike. Select Battle Maps and purchase Advance Warpaper. Select Display from the Design Room and choose Classic 1.

HACHI'S LAND

Insert Advance Wars in the GBA slot of your Nintendo DS. Start Advance Wars: Dual Strike. Select Battle Maps and purchase Hachi's Land for 1.

NELL'S LAND

Insert Advance Wars in the GBA slot of your Nintendo DS. Start Advance Wars: Dual Strike. Select Battle Maps and purchase Nell's Land for 1.

ADVANCE WARPAPER 2

Insert Advance Wars 2: Black Hole Rising in the GBA slot of your Nintendo DS. Start Advance Wars: Dual Strike. Select Battle Maps and purchase Advance Warpaper 2. Select Display from the Design Room and choose Classic 2.

LASH'S LAND

Insert Advance Wars 2: Black Hole Rising in the GBA slot of your Nintendo DS. Start Advance Wars: Dual Strike. Select Battle Maps and purchase Lash's Land for 1.

STRUM'S LAND

Insert Advance Wars 2: Black Hole Rising in the GBA slot of your Nintendo DS. Start Advance Wars: Dual Strike. Select Battle Maps and purchase Strum's Land for 1.

ANIMANIACS: LIGHTS, CAMERA, ACTION!

SKIP LEVEL

Pause the game and press L, L, R, R, Down, Down.

DISABLE TIME

Pause the game and press L, R, Left, Left, Up, Up.

KINGSIZE PICKUPS

Pause the game and press Right, Right, Right, Left, Left, Left, R, L.

PASSWORDS

LEVEL	PASSWORD	LEVEL	PASSWORD
1	Wakko, Wakko, Wakko, Wakko, Wakko	9	Dot, Dot, Yakko, Pinky, Wakko
2	Dot, Yakko, Brain, Wakko, Pinky	10	Brain, Dot, Brain, Yakko, Wakko
3	Yakko, Dot, Wakko, Wakko, Brain	11	Akko, Yakko, Pinky, Dot, Dot
4	Pinky, Yakko, Yakko, Dot, Brain	12	Pinky, Pinky, Brain, Dot, Wakko
5	Pinky, Pinky, Yakko, Wakko, Wakko	13	Yakko, Wakko, Pinky, Wakko, Brain
6	Brain, Dot, Brain, Pinky, Yakko	14	Pinky, Wakko, Brain, Wakko, Yakko
7	Brain, Pinky, Wakko, Pinky, Brain	15	Dot, Pinky, Wakko, Wakko, Yakko
8	Brain Pinky, Pinky, Wakko, Wakko		

ASPHALT URBAN GT

MONEY FOR NOTHING

Buy the Chevrolet 2005 Corvette C6 for $45,000. Then, go to your garage and sell it for $45,500.

BEN 10: PROTECTOR OF EARTH

GWEN 10 SKINS

At the level select, press Left, Right, Left, Right, L, R, Select.

GALACTIC ENFORCER SKINS

At the level select, press A, B, X, Y, L, R, Select.

ULTRA BEN SKINS

At the level select, press Up, Right, Down, Left, A, B, Select.

BRAIN AGE: TRAIN YOUR BRAIN IN MINUTES A DAY

BRAIN AGE CHECK SELECTION MENU

At the Daily Training Menu, hold Select while choosing Brain Age Check.

TOP 3 LISTS

At the Daily Training Menu, hold Select while choosing Graph.

BRAIN VOYAGE

ALL GOLD MEDALS

At the World Map, press A, B, Up, L, L, Y.

INFINITE COINS

At the World Tour Mode, press L, Up, X, Up, R, Y.

BUBBLE BOBBLE REVOLUTION

BONUS LEVELS IN CLASSIC MODE

At the Classic mode Title screen, press L, R, L, R, L, R, Right, Select. Touch the door at Level 20.

POWER UP! MODE IN CLASSIC VERSION

At the Classic mode Title screen, press Select, R, L, Left, Right, R, Select, Right.

SUPER BUBBLE BOBBLE IN CLASSIC VERSION

You must first defeat the boss with two players. At the Classic mode Title screen, press Left, R, Left, Select, Left, L, Left, Select.

BUILD-A-BEAR WORKSHOP

At the Select a Slot screen, press Up, Up, Down, Down, Left, Right, Left, Right, B, A. Now you can enter the following codes:

ALL LEVELS
At the level select, hold L + R.

ALL ACTIVITIES
At the workshop screen, press R.

ALL MOVES
At the garden screen, press L.

BUST-A-MOVE DS

DARK WORLD
First you must complete the game. At the Title screen, press A Left Right A.

SOUND TEST
At the Main menu, press Select, A, B, Left, Right, A, Select, Right.

CODE LYOKO

CODELYOKO.COM SECRET FILES
Enter the following as Secret Codes on the My Secret Album page of www.codelyoko.com:

SECRET FILE	CODE
Dark Enemies Wallpaper	9L8Q
Desert Sketch	6G7T
Fight Video	4M9P
FMV Ending	5R5K
Forest Sketch	8C3X
Ice Sketch	2F6U
Mountain Sketch	7E5V
Overbike	3Q4L

SECRET FILE	CODE
Overboard	8P3M
Overwing	8N2N
Scorpion Video	9H8S
Scorpion Wallpaper	3D4W
Sector 5 Sketch	5J9R
Ulrich	9A9Z
Yumi	4B2Y

DRAGLADE

CHARACTERS

CHARACTER	TO UNLOCK
Asuka	Defeat Daichi's story
Gyamon	Defeat Guy's story
Koki	Defeat Hibito's story
Shura	Defeat Kairu's story

HIDDEN QUEST: SHADOW OF DARKNESS
Defeat Story Mode with all of the main characters. This unlocks the hidden quest in Synethesia.

ZEKE
Complete all of the quests including Shadow of Darkness to unlock Zeke in wireless battle.

DRAGON QUEST HEROES: ROCKET SLIME

KNIGHTRO TANK IN MULTIPLAYER

While in the church, press Y, L, L, Y, R, R, Y, Up, Down, Select.

THE NEMESIS TANK IN MULTIPLAYER

While in the church, press Y, R, R, up, L, L, Y, Down, Down, Down, Y, Select.

DRAGON QUEST MONSTERS: JOKER

CAPTAIN CROW

As you travel between the islands on the sea scooters, you are occasionally attacked by pirates. Discover the route on which the pirates are located at the bulletin board in any scoutpost den. When you face them between Infant Isle and Celeste Isle, Captain Crow makes an appearance. Defeat him and he forces himself into your team.

SOLITAIRE'S CHALLENGE

After completing the main game, load your game again for a new endeavor. The hero is in Solitaire's office, where she proposes a new nonstop challenge known as Solitaire's Challenge.

METAL KING SLIME

Acquire 100 different skills for your library and talk to the woman in Solitaire's office.

METAL KAISER SLIME

Acquire 150 different skills for your library and talk to the woman in Solitaire's office.

LEOPOLD

Acquire all of the skills for your library and talk to the woman in Solitaire's office.

LIQUID METAL SLIME

Collect 100 monsters in your library and talk to the man in Solitaire's office.

GRANDPA SLIME

Collect 200 monsters in your library and talk to the man in Solitaire's office.

EMPYREA

Collect all of the monsters in your library and talk to the man in Solitaire's office.

TRODE AND ROBBIN' HOOD

Complete both the skills and monster libraries and talk to both the man and woman in Solitaire's office.

DRAWN TO LIFE

HEAL ALL DAMAGE

During a game, press Start, hold L and press Y, X, Y, X, Y, X, A.

INVINCIBLITY

During a game, press Start, hold L and press A, X, B, B, Y.

ALIEN TEMPLATES

During a game, press Start, hold L and press X, Y, B, A, A.

ANIMAL TEMPLATES

During a game, press Start, hold L and press B, B, A, A, X.

8

ROBOT TEMPLATES
During a game, press Start, hold L and press Y, X, Y, X, A.

SPORTS TEMPLATES
During a game, press Start, hold L and press Y, A, B, A, X.

DRAWN TO LIFE: SPONGEBOB SQUAREPANTS EDITION

9,999,999 COINS
Select Cheat Entry and enter Down, Down, B, B, Down, Left, Up, Right, A.

FINAL FANTASY FABLES: CHOCOBO TALES

OMEGA—WAVE CANNON CARD
Select Send from the Main menu and then choose Download Pop-Up Card. Press L, L, Up, B, B, Left.

GODZILLA UNLEASHED: DOUBLE SMASH

ANGUIRUS
Defeat Hedorah Terrorizes San Francisco.

DESTOROYAH
Defeat Monster Island, The Final Battle.

FIRE RODAN
Defeat Biollante Attacks Paris.

KING GHIDORAH
Defeat Mecha King Ghidorah Ravages Bangkok.

GRID

UNLOCK ALL
Select Cheat Codes from the Options and enter 233558.

INVULNERABILITY
Select Cheat Codes from the Options and enter 161650.

DRIFT MASTER
Select Cheat Codes from the Options and enter 789520.

PERFECT GRIP
Select Cheat Codes from the Options and enter 831782.

HIGH ROLLER
Select Cheat Codes from the Options and enter 401134.

GHOST CAR
Select Cheat Codes from the Options and enter 657346.

TOY CARS
Select Cheat Codes from the Options and enter 592014.

MM MODE
Select Cheat Codes from the Options and enter 800813.

IZUNA: LEGEND OF THE UNEMPLOYED NINJA

PATH OF TRAILS BONUS DUNGEON

After completing the game, touch the crystal from the beginning.

JAKE HUNTER: DETECTIVE CHRONICLES

PASSWORDS

Select Password from the main menu and enter the following:

UNLOCKABLE	PASSWORD
1 Password Info	AAAA
2 Visuals	LEET
3 Visuals	GONG
4 Visuals	CARS
5 Movies	ROSE
6 Jukebox	BIKE
7 Hints	HINT

JAM SESSIONS

BONUS SONGS

At the Free Play menu, press Up, Up, Down, Down, Left, Right, Left, Right. This unlocks I'm Gonna Miss Her by Brad Paisley, Needles and Pins by Tom Petty, and Wild Thing by Jimi Hendrix.

KIRBY: CANVAS CURSE

JUMP GAME

Defeat the game with all five characters. Select the game file to get Jump Game next to the options on the Main menu.

KONAMI CLASSICS SERIES: ARCADE HITS

GRADIUS

ALL POWER-UPS EXCEPT SPEED

At the Gradius title screen, press Up, Up, Down, Down, Left, Right, Left, Right, B, A. After starting a game, press Start to get every power-up except Speed. This code can be entered only once.

LEGO BATMAN

You should hear a confirmation sound after the following codes are entered.

ALL CHARACTERS

At the main menu, press X, Up, B, Down, Y, Left, Start, Right, R, R, L, R, R, Down, Down, Up, Y, Y, Start, Select.

ALL EPISODES AND FREE PLAY MODE

At the main menu, press Right, Up, R, L, X, Y, Right, Left, B, L, R, L, Down, Down, Up, Y, Y, X, X, B, B, Up, Up, L, R, Start, Select.

ALL EXTRAS

At the main menu, press Up, Down, L, R, L, R, L, Left, Right, X, X, Y, Y, B, B, L, Up, Down, L, R, L, R, Up, Up, Down, Start, Select.

1 MILLION STUDS

At the main menu, press X, Y, B, B, Y, X, L, L, R, R, Up, Down, Left, Right, Start, Select.

3 MILLION STUDS

At the main menu, press Up, Up, B, Down, Down, X, Left, Left, Y, L, R, L, R, B, Y, X, Start, Select.

LEGO INDIANA JONES: THE ORIGINAL ADVENTURES

You should hear a confirmation sound after the following codes are entered.

ALL CHARACTERS

At the title screen, press X, Up, B, Down, Y, Left, Start, Right, R, R, L, R, R, Down, Down, Up, Y, Y, Y, Start, Select.

ALL EPISODES AND FREE PLAY MODE

Right, Up, R, L, X, Y, Right, Left, B, L, R, L, Down, Down, Up, Y, Y, X, X, B, B, Up, Up, L, R, Start, Select.

ALL EXTRAS

Up, Down, L, R, L, R, L, Left, Right, X, X, Y, Y, B, B, L, Up, Down, L, R, L, R, Up, Up, Down, Start, Select.

1,000,000 STUDS

At the title screen, press X, Y, B, B, Y, X, L, L, R, R, Up, Down, Left, Right, Start, Select.

3,000,000 STUDS

At the title screen, press Up, Up, B, Down, Down, X, Left, Left, Y, L, R, L, R, B, Y, X, Start, Select.

LEGO STAR WARS II: THE ORIGINAL TRILOGY

10 STUDS

At the Mos Eisley cantina, enter 4PR28U.

OBI WAN GHOST

At the Mos Eisley cantina, enter BEN917.

LEGO STAR WARS: THE COMPLETE SAGA

3,000,000 STUDS

At the main menu, press Start, Start, Down, Down, Left, Left, Up, Up, Select. This cheat can only be used once.

DEBUG MENUS

At the main menu, press Up, Left, Down, Right, Up, Left, Down, Right, Up, Left, Down, Right, R, L, Start, Select.

BONUS TOUCH GAME 1

At the main menu, press Up, Up, Down, L, L, R, R.

LOCK'S QUEST

REPLACE CLOCKWORKS WITH KINGDOM FORCE
After completing the game, hold R and select your profile.

ENDING STORY
After completing the game, hold L and select your profile.

LUNAR KNIGHTS

SOUND DATA (BOKTAI)
With Boktai in the GBA slot, purchase this from the General Store in Acuna.

SOUND DATA (BOKTAI 2)
With Boktai 2 in the GBA slot, purchase this from the General Store in Acuna.

MARIO PARTY DS

BOSS BASH
Complete Story Mode.

EXPERT CPU DIFFICULTY LEVEL
Complete Story Mode.

MUSIC AND VOICE ROOM
Complete Story Mode.

SCORE SCUFFLE
Complete Story Mode.

TRIANGLE TWISTER PUZZLE MODE
Complete Story Mode.

METROID PRIME PINBALL

PHAZON MINES
Complete Omega Pirate in Multi Mission mode.

PHENDRANA DRIFTS
Complete Thardus in Multi Mission mode.

MY WORD COACH

WORD POPPERS MINIGAME
After reaching 200 word successes, at the options menu, press A, B, X, Y, A, B.

N+

ATARI BONUS LEVELS
Select Unlockables from the main menu, hold L + R and press A, B, A, B, A, A, B.

NAMCO MUSEUM DS

DIG-DUG 2 OLD VERSION

From the Dig Dug 2 menu, select Hardcore Options from the Settings. Change New Version to Old.

SECRET GAME: SUPER XEVIOUS

From the Xevious menu, select Hardcore Options from the Settings. Change the version to Super Xevious.

NARUTO: PATH OF THE NINJA

After defeating the game, talk to Knohamaru on the roof of the Ninja Academy. He allows you go get certain cheats by tapping four successive spots on the touch screen in order. There are 12 different spots on the screen. We have numbered them from left to right, top to bottom, as follows:

1	2	3	4
5	6	7	8
9	10	11	12

Enter the following codes by touching the four spots in the order listed.

UNLOCK	CODE
4th Hokage's Sword	4, 7, 11, 5
Fuji Fan	8, 11, 2, 5
Jiraiya	11, 3, 1, 6
Rajin's Sword	7, 6, 5, 11
Rasengan	9, 2, 12, 7

NARUTO: PATH OF THE NINJA 2

CHARACTER PASSWORDS

Talk to Konohamaru at the school to enter the following passwords. You must first complete the game for the passwords to work.

CHARACTER	PASSWORD
Gaara	D K F I A B J L
Gai	I K A G D E F L
Iruka	J G D L K A I B
Itachi Uchiha	G B E I D A L F
Jiraiya	E B J D A G F L
Kankuro	A L J K B E D G
Kyuubi Naruto	G J H L B F D E
Orochimaru	A H F B L E J G
Temari	H F I C L K B G
The Third Hokage	C G H A J B E L

MISSION PASSWORDS

Talk to Konohamaru at the school to enter the following passwords. You must first complete the game for the passwords to work.

MISSION	PASSWORD
An Extreme Battle!	H L B A K G C D
The Legendary Haze Ninja!	F G E H I D A L
The Legendary Sannin!	B C E G K F H L

NEED FOR SPEED CARBON: OWN THE CITY

INFINITE NITROUS
At the Main menu, press Up, Up, Down, Left, A, B, B, A.

NEW SUPER MARIO BROS.

PLAY AS LUIGI IN SINGLE PLAYER
At the Select a File screen, hold L + R while selecting a saved game.

SECRET CHALLENGE MODE
On the map, pause the game and press L, R, L, R, X, X, Y, Y.

THE NEW YORK TIMES CROSSWORDS

BLACK & WHITE
At the Main menu, press Up, Up, Down, Down, B, B, Y, Y.

NICKTOONS: ATTACK OF THE TOYBOTS

DANNY PHANTOM 2
Select Unlock Code from the Options and enter Tak, Jimmy, Zim, El Tigre.

SPONGEBOB 2
Select Unlock Code from the Options and enter Patrick, Jenny, Timmy, Tak.

NICKTOONS: BATTLE FOR VOLCANO ISLAND

FRUIT BECOMES TOYS IN FRUIT COLLECTING MINI-GAME
Select Unlock Codes from the Options and enter Spongebob, Danny, Timmy, Cosmo.

PAC-PIX

BUTTERFLY HIDDEN GESTURE
Select Sketchbook from the Gallery. Draw a figure eight. The drawing should fly upwards.

CHERRIES HIDDEN GESTURE

Select Sketchbook from the Gallery. Draw a pair of cherries starting with one of the circles.

POGO STICK HIDDEN GESTURE

Select Sketchbook from the Gallery. Draw a P and it will bounce off the screen.

RAIN CLOUD HIDDEN GESTURE

Select Sketchbook from the Gallery. Draw a cloud and it will turn blue and rain will fall from the drawing.

SNAKE HIDDEN GESTURE

Select Sketchbook from the Gallery. Draw an a squiggly line. It will turn green and slither away.

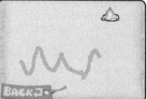

TREBLE CLEF HIDDEN GESTURE

Select Sketchbook from the Gallery. Draw a treble clef.

SHOOT ARROWS AT PAC-MAN

After you have earned the Arrow gesture in Chapter 4, select Sketchbook from the Gallery. Draw an arrow facing Pac-man.

PIRATES OF THE CARIBBEAN: DEAD MAN'S CHEST

10 GOLD

During a game, press Right, X, X, Right, Left.

INVINCIBILITY

During a game, press Up, Down, Left, Right (x5), Left, Right, Up, Down, Left, Right, Up (x5), Left.

UNLIMITED POWER

During a game, press Up, Up, Down, Down, Left, Right, Left, Right, L, R.

RESTORE HEALTH

During a game, press Y, Y, Select, Left, Right, Left, Right, Left.

RESTORE SAVVY

During a game, press X, X, Select, Up, Down, Up, Down, Up.

GHOST FORM MODE
During a game, press Y, X, Y, X, Y, X.

SEASICKNESS MODE
During a game, press X, X, Y, X, X, Y.

SILLY WEAPONS
During a game, press Y, Y, X, Y (x3).

AXE
During a game, press Left, L, L, Down, Down, Left, Up, Up, Down, Down.

BLUNDERBUSS
During a game, press Down, L, L, Down (x3).

CHICKEN
During a game, press Right, L, L, Up, Down, Down.

EXECUTIONER AXE
During a game, press Right, L, L, Up, Down, Up, Right, Right, Left(x2).

PIG
During a game, press Right, R, R, Down, Up, Up.

PISTOL
During a game, press Down, L, L, Down, Down, Right.

RIFLE
During a game, press Left, L, L, Up (x3).

FAST MUSIC
During a game, press Y, Select, Y (x4).

SLOW MUSIC
During a game, press Y, Select, X (x4).

DISABLE CHEATS
During a game, press X (x6).

PRINCESS NATASHA

ALL GADGETS
Select Codes from the Extras menu and enter OLEGSGIZMO.

EXTRA LEVELS
Select Codes from the Extras menu and enter SMASHROBOT.

INFINITE LIVES
Select Codes from the Extras menu and enter CRUSHLUBEK.

PUYO POP FEVER

ALL CHARACTERS AND CUTSCENES
Select Gallery from the Options. Highlight cutscene viewer, hold X and press Up, Down, Left, Right.

RACE DRIVER: CREATE & RACE

ALL CHALLENGES
Select Cheat Codes from Extras and enter 942785.

ALL CHAMPIONSHIPS
Select Cheat Codes from Extras and enter 761492.

ALL REWARDS
Select Cheat Codes from Extras and enter 112337.

FREE DRIVE
Select Cheat Codes from Extras and enter 171923.

NO DAMAGE

Select Cheat Codes from Extras and enter 505303.

EASY STEERING

Select Cheat Codes from Extras and enter 611334.

MINIATURE CARS

Select Cheat Codes from Extras and enter 374288.

MM VIEW

Select Cheat Codes from Extras and enter 467348.

RIDGE RACER DS

00-AGENT CAR

Finish more than ten races in multi-player.

CADDY CAR

Finish more than ten races in multi-player.

GALAGA '88 CAR

Finish more than ten races in multi-player.

MARIO RACING CAR

Finish more than ten races in multi-player.

POOKA CAR

Finish more than ten races in multi-player.

RED SHIRT RAGE CAR

Finish more than ten races in multi-player.

SHY GUY CAR

Finish more than ten races in multi-player.

GALAGA PAC JAM SONG

Unlock the Pooka car.

MUSHROOM KINGDOM II SONG

Unlock the DK Team Racing car.

SIMCITY CREATOR

99999999 MONEY

Enter MONEYBAGS as a password.

AMERICAN PROSPERITY AGE MAP

Enter NEWWORLD as a password.

ASIA AGE MAP

Enter SAMURAI as a password.

ASIA AGE BONUS MAP

Enter FEUDAL as a password.

DAWN OF CIVILIZATION MAP

Enter ANCIENT as a password.

GLOBAL WARMING MAP

Enter MODERN as a password.

GLOBAL WARMING BONUS MAP

Enter BEYOND as a password.

RENAISSANCE BONUS MAP

Enter HEREANDNOW as a password.

SIMCITY DS

LANDMARK BUILDINGS

Select Landmark Collection from the Museum menu. Choose Password and enter the following:

BUILDING	PASSWORD	BUILDING	PASSWORD
Anglican Cathedral (UK)	kipling	Mt. Fuji (Japan)	hiroshige
Arc de Triomphe (France)	gaugin	National Museum (Taiwan)	yuantlee
Atomic Dome (Japan)	kawabata	Neuschwanstein Castle (Germany)	beethoven
Big Ben (UK)	orwell	Notre Dame (France)	hugo
Bowser Castle (Nintendo)	hanafuda	Palace of Fine Arts (USA)	bunche
Brandenburg Gate (Germany)	gropius	Palacio Real (Spain)	cervantes
Coit Tower	kerouac	Paris Opera (France)	daumier
Conciergerie (France)	rodin	Parthenon (Greece)	callas
Daibutsu (Japan)	mishima	Pharos of Alexandria (Egypt)	zewail
Edo Castle (Japan)	shonagon	Rama IX Royal Park (Thailand)	phu
Eiffel Tower (France)	camus	Reichstag (Germany)	goethe
Gateway Arch (USA)	twain	Sagrada Familia (Spain)	dali
Grand Central Station (USA)	f.scott	Shuri Castle (Japan)	basho
Great Pyramids (Egypt)	mahfouz	Smithsonian Castle (USA)	pauling
Hagia Sofia (Turkey)	ataturk	Sphinx (Egypt)	haykal
Helsinki Cathedral (Finland)	kivi	St Paul's Cathedral (UK)	defoe
Himeji Castle (Japan)	hokusai	St. Basil's Cathedral (Russia)	tolstoy
Holstentor (Germany)	durer	St. Stephen's Cathedral (Austria)	mozart
Independence Hall (USA)	mlkingjr	Statue of Liberty (USA)	pollack
Jefferson Memorial (USA)	thompson	Stockholm Palace (Sweden)	bergman
Kokkai (Japan)	soseki	Taj Mahal (India)	tagore
LA Landmark (USA)	hemingway	Tower of London (UK)	maugham
Lincoln Memorial (USA)	melville	Trafalgar Square (UK)	joyce
Liver Building (UK)	dickens	United Nations (UN)	amnesty
Melbourne Cricket Ground (Australia)	damemelba	United States Capitol (USA)	poe
		Washington Monument	capote
Metropolitan Cath. (UK)	austen	Westminster Abbey (UK)	greene
Moai (Chile)	allende	White House (USA)	Steinbeck

THE SIMS 2

MONGOO MONKEY FOR THE CASINO

Start the game with Sims 2 in the GBA slot of your Nintendo DS.

SOUL BUBBLES

REVEAL ALL CALABASH LOCATIONS

Pause the game and press A, L, L, R, A, Down, A, R.

ALL LEVELS

At the World Select, press L, Up, X, Up, R, Y.

ALL GALLERY ITEMS

At the Gallery, press B, Up, B, B, L, Y.

CARD INPUT SYSTEM

When the Upsilon Cube is unearthed and shown to Aldous, the Card Input System feature becomes available. This will allow you to input data from Spectrobe Cards. These give you new Spectrobes and Custom Parts. If you get your hands on a Spectrobe Card and the system is unlocked, investigate the card input system in the spaceship's lower deck. Follow the instructions on the upper screen to match the four corner points of the card to the corners of the touch screen. Touch the screen through the seven holes in the card in the order indicated on the card. If the code you input is correct, you receive Spectrobes, custom Parts, minerals or Cubes.

You can input the same card a maximum of four times. This means that you can only obtain four of the same Spectrobes from a single card. You can only input cards once. And some cards cannot be input until you have reached a certain point in the game.

The following table gives you a seven character code which refers to the spots you touch in order. The first four characters have you touching the four corners and the final three are spots among the 12 in the middle. To get Cyclone Geo, Hammer Geo, Ice Geo, Plasma Geo, or Thunder Geo, you must first beat the game.

EFFECT	CODE	EFFECT	CODE
Aobasat Apex	BACD HEP	Samurite Voltar	BACD LHM
Cyclone Geo	CDAB LGM	Sapphire Mineral	ABDC FJO
Danaphant Tuska	ABDC ELI	Segulos Propos	CDAB KIH
Danilob	DABC GLO	Seguslice	CDAB GKP
Emerald Mineral	BACD FKN	Shakor Bristle	DABC MLK
Grilden Biblad	ABDC FIH	Sigma Cube	CDAB PML
Grildragos Drafly	CDAB MHK	Tau Cube	DABC LIF
Gristar	BACD EJN	Thunder Geo	DABC MEL
Hammer Geo	ABDC ELH	Vilagrisp (Custom Part)	DABC EIN
Harumitey Lazos	DABC ILM	Vilakroma	BACD NLM
Ice Geo	CDAB HEK	Vilakroma (Custom Color 1)	CDAB LJI
Inataflare Auger	ABDC IGH	Vilakroma (Custom Color 2)	DABC EGP
Inkalade	ABDC GLP	Windora	ABDC MGP
Iota Cube	ABDC OHE	Windora (Custom Color 1)	DABC EHG
Komainu	CDAB HMJ	Windora (Custom Color 2)	CDAB JPM
Kugaster Sonara	DABC LOE	Windora Ortex	BACD IPG
Mossax Jetspa (Custom Color 1)	BACD JML	Windora Ortex (Custom Color 1)	ABDC MPH
Naglub	ABDC EJM	Windora Ortex (Custom Color 2)	DABC MGH
Plasma Geo	BACD KLE	Windora Sordina	CDAB PEO
Rho Cube	BACD PNI	Windora Sordina (Custom Color 1)	BACD MOH
Ruby Mineral	CDAB FKO	Windora Sordina (Custom Color 2)	ABDC LEN
Samukabu	ABDC OIL	Wing Geo (must beat game	DABC MNP

SPIDER-MAN 2

ALL SPECIAL MOVES
Load the game with Spider-Man: Mysterio's Menace for Game Boy Advance in the Nintendo DS.

STAR TREK: TACTICAL ASSAULT

KLINGON CAMPAIGN
At the Main menu, press Up, Down, Left, Right, Select, Start, X.

UNLOCK MISSIONS
At the Main menu, press Up, Down, Left, Right, Select, Start, Start.

EXTRA CREW UPGRADES
At the Main menu, press Up, Down, Left, Right, Select, Start, Select.

ALL SHIPS IN SKIRMISH AND MULTIPLAYER
At the Main menu, press Up, Down, Left, Right, Select, Start, Y.

ANY SHIP IN MISSIONS
At the Main menu, press Up, Down, Left, Right, Select, Start, B.

STAR WARS EPISODE III: REVENGE OF THE SITH

MASTER DIFFICULTY
Defeat the game.

ANAKIN'S STARFIGHTER
Beat the Anakin bot in multiplayer.

DARTH VADER'S TIE FIGHTER
Defeat the Darth Vader bot in multiplayer.

GENERAL GREVIOUS'S STARFIGHTER
Defeat the General Grevious bot in multiplayer.

MILLENIUM FALCON
Defeat the Solo bot in multiplayer.

SLAVE I
Defeat the Fett bot in multiplayer.

X-WING
Defeat the Luke bot in multiplayer.

STAR WARS: THE FORCE UNLEASHED

INCREASED HEALTH
Select Unleashed Codes from the Extras menu and enter QSSPVENXO.

MAX OUT FORCE POWERS
Select Unleashed Codes from the Extras menu and enter CPLOOLKBF.

UNLIMITED FORCE ENERGY
Select Unleashed Codes from the Extras menu and enter TVENCVMJZ.

MORE POWERFUL LIGHTSABER
Select Unleashed Codes from the Extras menu and enter lightsaber.

UBER LIGHTSABER
Select Unleashed Codes from the Extras menu and enter MOMIROXIW.

ROM KOTA
Select Unleashed Codes from the Extras menu and enter mandalore.

CEREMONIAL JEDI ROBES
Select Unleashed Codes from the Extras menu and enter CURSEZRUX.

DAD'S ROBES
Select Unleashed Codes from the Extras menu and enter wookiee.

DARTH VADER'S COSTUME

Select Unleashed Codes from the Extras menu and enter HRMXRKVEN.

KENTO'S ROBE

Select Unleashed Codes from the Extras menu and enter KBVMSEVNM.

KOTA'S OUTFIT

Select Unleashed Codes from the Extras menu and enter EEDOPVENG.

SITH ROBE

Select Unleashed Codes from the Extras menu and enter ZWSFVENXA.

SITH ROBES

Select Unleashed Codes from the Extras menu and enter holocron.

SITH STALKER ARMOR

Select Unleashed Codes from the Extras menu and enter CPLZKMZTD.

TAMAGOTCHI CONNECTION: CORNER SHOP 3

DOUBLE LAYERED CAKE

Select Enter Code from the Special menu and enter R6194BJD6F.

TEENAGE MUTANT NINJA TURTLES 3: MUTANT NIGHTMARE

CRYSTALS ARE EASTER EGGS

Select Input Password from the Options and enter SRDSLLMS.

CRYSTALS ARE JACK-O-LANTERNS

Select Input Password from the Options and enter DRSSMRLD.

CRYSTALS ARE SANTAS

Select Input Password from the Options and enter LLDMSRMD.

LIFE ICONS ARE PIZZA

Select Input Password from the Options and enter DDRMLRDS.

COWABUNGA

At the Title screen, press U, U, D, D, L, R, L, R, B, A.

TIGER WOODS PGA TOUR 2005

EMERALD DRAGON

Earn $1,000,000.

GREEK ISLES

Earn $1,500,000.

PARADISE COVER

Earn $2,000,000.

EA SPORTS FAVORITES

Earn $5,000,000

MEAN8TEEN

Earn $10,000,000.

FANTASY SPECIALS

Earn $15,000,000.

LEGEND COMPILATION 1

Defeat Hogan in Legend Tour.

LEGEND COMPILATION 2

Defeat Gary Player in Legend Tour.

LEGEND COMPILATION 3

Defeat Ballesteros in Legend Tour.

LEGEND COMPILATION 4

Defeat Palmer in Legend Tour.

LEGEND COMPILATION 5

Defeat Nicklaus in Legend Tour.

THE HUSTLER'S DREAM 18

Defeat The Hustler in Legend Tour.

TIGER'S DREAM 18

Defeat Tiger Woods in Legend Tour.

TOM CLANCY'S SPLINTER CELL CHAOS THEORY

UNLIMITED AMMO/GADGETS

Defeat the game.

CHARACTER SKINS

Defeat the game.

TONY HAWK'S DOWNHILL JAM

ALWAYS SNOWSKATE

Select Buy Stuff from the Skateshop. Choose Enter Code and enter SNOWSK8T.

MIRRORED MAPS

Select Buy Stuff from the Skateshop. Choose Enter Code and enter MIRRORBALL.

ABOMINABLE SNOWMAN OUTFIT

Select Buy Stuff from the Skateshop. Choose Enter Code and enter BIGSNOWMAN.

ZOMBIE SKATER OUTFIT

Select Buy Stuff from the Skateshop. Choose Enter Code and enter ZOMBIEALIVE.

TRAUMA CENTER: UNDER THE KNIFE

X1: KYRIAKI MISSION

Defeat the game. Find the X Missions under Challenge Mode.

X2: DEFTERA MISSION

Defeat X1 : Kyriaki Mission. Find the X Missions under Challenge Mode.

X3: TRITI MISSION

Defeat X2 : Deftera Mission. Find the X Missions under Challenge Mode.

X4: TETARTI MISSION

Defeat X3 : Triti Mission. Find the X Missions under Challenge Mode.

X5: PEMPTI MISSION

Defeat X4 : Tetarti Mission. Find the X Missions under Challenge Mode.

X6: PARAKEVI MISSION

Defeat X5 : Pempti Mission. Find the X Missions under Challenge Mode.

X7: SAVATO MISSION

Defeat X6 : Parakevi Mission. Find the X Missions under Challenge Mode.

THE URBZ: SIMS IN THE CITY

CLUB XIZZLE

Once you gain access to Club Xizzle, enter with the password "bucket."

WORLD CHAMPIONSHIP POKER

UNLOCK CASINOS

At the Title screen, press Y, X, Y, B, L, R. Then press the following direction:

DIRECTION	CASINO
Left	Amazon
Right	Nebula
Down	Renaissance

YU-GI-OH! NIGHTMARE TROUBADOUR

CREDITS

Unlock the Password Machine by defeating the Expert Cup. Enter the Duel Shop and select the Slot maching. Enter 00000375.

SOUND TEST

Unlock the Password Machine by defeating the Expert Cup. Enter the Duel Shop and select the Slot maching. Enter 57300000.

YU-GI-OH! WORLD CHAMPIONSHIP 2008

CARD PASSWORDS

Enter the following in the password machine to receive the corresponding card. You must already have the card to use the password.

PASSWORD EFFECT

CARD	PASSWORD	CARD	PASSWORD
7	67048711	Amplifier	00303660
7 Colored Fish	23771716	Anti-Spell	53112492
7 Completed	86198326	Aqua Madoor	85639257
A Feint Plan	68170903	Aqua Spirit	40916023
A Hero Emerges	21597117	Archfiend of Gilfer	50287060
Abyss Soldier	18318842	Armed Changer	90374791
Acid Rain	21323861	Armed Ninja	09076207
Acid Trap Hole	41356845	Armored Glass	21070956
Adhesive Explosive	53828196	Armored Zombie	20277860
Agido	16135253	Array of Revealing Light	69296555
Airknight Parshath	18036057	Arsenal Bug	42364374
Aitsu	48202661	Arsenal Robber	55348096
Alkana Knight Joker	06150044	Assault on GHQ	62633180
Alligator's Sword	64428736	Asura Priest	02134346
Alligator's Sword Dragon	03366982	Attack and Receive	63689843
Alpha the Magnet Warrior	99785935	Autonomous Action Unit	71453557
Altar for Tribute	21070956	Axe of Despair	40619825
Amazon Archer	91869203	Axe Raider	48305365
Amazoness Archers	67987611	B. Skull Dragon	11901678
Amazoness Blowpiper	73574678	Baby Dragon	88819587
Amazoness Chain Master	29654737	Back to Square One	47453433
Amazoness Fighter	55821894	Backfire	82705573
Amazoness Paladin	47480070	Bad Reaction to Simochi	40633297
Amazoness Spellcaster	81325903	Bait Doll	07165085
Amazoness Swords Woman	94004268	Ballista of Rampart Smashing	00242146
Amazoness Tiger	10979723	Banisher of the Light	61528025
Amphibian Beast	67371383	Banner of Courage	10012614

CARD	PASSWORD	CARD	PASSWORD
Bark of The Dark Ruler	41925941	Card Destruction	72892473
Baron of the Fiend Sword	86325596	Card of Sanctity	04266498
Barrel Behind the Door	78783370	Card Shuffle	12183332
Barrel Dragon	81480460	Castle of Dark Illusions	00062121
Battery Charger	61181383	Castle Walls	44209392
Batteryman AA	63142001	Catapult Turtle	95727991
Batteryman C	19733961	Ceasefire	36468556
Batteryman D	55401221	Celtic Guardian	91152256
Battle Ox	05053103	Cemetery Bomb	51394546
Battle Warrior	55550921	Centrifugal Field	01801154
Beast Fangs	46009906	Cestus of Dagla	28106077
Beast Soul Swap	35149085	Chain Destruction	01248895
Beastking of the Swamps	99426834	Chain Disappearance	57139487
Beautiful Headhuntress	16899564	Chain Energy	79323590
Beckoning Light	16255442	Chaos Command Magician	72630549
Berfomet	77207191	Chaos End	61044390
Berserk Gorilla	39168895	Chaos Greed	97439308
Beta the Magnet Warrior	39256679	Chimera the Flying Mythical Beast	04796100
Bickuribox	25655502	Chiron the Mage	16956455
Big Bang Shot	61127349	Chorus of Sanctuary	81380218
Big Eye	16768387	Chthonian Alliance	46910446
Big Shield Gardna	65240384	Chthonian Blast	18271561
Birdface	45547649	Chthonian Polymer	72287557
Black Illusion Ritual	41426869	Clay Charge	22479888
Black Luster Ritual	55761792	Cocoon of Evolution	40240595
Black Luster Soldier	72989439	Coffin Seller	65830223
Black Magic Ritual	76792184	Cold Wave	60682203
Black Pendant	65169794	Command Knight	10375182
Bladefly	28470714	Conscription	31000575
Blast Held by a Tribute	89041555	Continuous Destruction Punch	68057622
Blast Magician	21051146	Contract with Exodia	33244944
Blast Sphere	26302522	Contract with the Dark Master	96420087
Blast with Chain	98239899	Convulsion of Nature	62966332
Blasting the Ruins	21466326	Copycat	26376390
Blessings of the Nile	30653173	Cosmo Queen	38999506
Blowback Dragon	25551951	Covering Fire	74458486
Blue Medicine	20871001	Crass Clown	93889755
Blue-Eyes Toon Dragon	53183600	Crawling Dragon #2	38289717
Blue-Eyes Ultimate Dragon	23995346	Crimson Sunbird	46696593
Blue-Eyes White Dragon	80906030	Crush Card Virus	57728570
Blue-Eyes White Dragon	80906030	Curse of Anubis	66742250
Book of Taiyou	38699854	Curse of Darkness	84970821
Bottomless Trap Hole	29401950	Curse of Dragon	28279543
Bowganian	52090844	Curse of the Masked Beast	94377247
Bracchio-Raidus	16507828	Cursed Seal of the Forbidden Spell	58851034
Brain Control	87910978	Cyber Raider	39978267
Breaker the Magical Warrior	71413901	Cyber Shield	63224564
Breath of Light	20101223	Cyber-Tech Alligator	48766543
Bright Castle	82878489	D.D. Borderline	60912752
Burning Land	24294108	D.D. Designator	33423043
Burning Spear	18937875	D.D. Assailant	70074904
Burst Return	27191436	D.D. Dynamite	08628798
Burst Stream of Destruction	17655904	D.D. Trap Hole	05606466
Buster Rancher	84740193	D.D. Warrior	37043180
Cannon Soldier	11384280	D.D. Warrior Lady	07572887
Cannonball Spear Shellfish	95614612	D. Tribe	02833249

CARD	PASSWORD
Dark Artist	72520073
Dark Deal	65824822
Dark Dust Spirit	89111398
Dark Elf	21417692
Dark Energy	04614116
Dark Factory of Mass Production	90928333
Dark Jeroid	90980792
Dark Magic Attack	02314238
Dark Magic Curtain	99789342
Dark Magician	46986414
Dark Magician Girl	38033121
Dark Magician of Chaos	40737112
Dark Master - Zorc	97642679
Dark Mimic LV1	74713516
Dark Mimic LV3	01102515
Dark Mirror Force	20522190
Dark Necrofear	31829185
Dark Paladin	98502113
Dark Rabbit	99261403
Dark Room of Nightmare	85562745
Dark Sage	92377303
Dark Snake Syndrome	47233801
Dark Spirit of the Silent	93599951
Dark World Lightning	93554166
Darkness Approaches	80168720
Dark-Piercing Light	45895206
Deck Devastation Virus	35027493
Decoy Dragon	02732323
Dedication through Light and Darkness	69542930
De-Fusion	95286165
Delta Attacker	39719977
Despair from the Dark	71200730
De-Spell	19159413
Destiny Board	94212438
Destruction Ring	21219755
Dian Keto the Cure Master	84257639
Dice Re-Roll	83241722
Different Dimension Capsule	11961740
Different Dimension Dragon	50939127
Different Dimension Gate	56460688
Diffusion Wave-Motion	87880531
Dimension Fusion	23557835
Dimension Wall	67095270
Dimensional Prison	70342110
Dimensionhole	22959079
Disappear	24623598
Disarmament	20727787
Divine Sword - Phoenix Blade	31423101
Divine Wrath	49010598
DNA Surgery	74701381
Doomcaliber Knight	78700060
Double Coston	44436472
Double Snare	03682106
Double Spell	24096228
Dragged Down into the Grave	16435235

CARD	PASSWORD
Dragon Capture Jar	50045299
Dragon Seeker	28563545
Dragon Treasure	01435851
Dragonic Attack	32437102
Dragon's Mirror	71490127
Draining Shield	43250041
Dramatic Rescue	80193355
Dream Clown	13215230
Drill Bug	88733579
Driving Snow	00473469
Drop Off	55773067
Dunames Dark Witch	12493482
Dust Barrier	31476755
Dust Tornado	60082867
Earth Chant	59820352
Earthbound Spirit's Invitation	65743242
Earthquake	82828051
Eatgaboon	42578427
Ectoplasmer	97342942
Ekibyo Drakmord	69954399
Electro-Whip	37820550
Elegant Egotist	90219263
Elemental Hero Avian	21844576
Elemental Hero Burstinatrix	58932615
Elemental Hero Clayman	84327329
Elemental Hero Flame Wingman	35809262
Elemental Hero Rampart Blaster	47737087
Elemental Hero Sparkman	20721928
Elemental Hero Thunder Giant	61204971
Embodiment of Apophis	28649820
Emergency Provisions	53046408
Enchanted Arrow	93260132
Enchanting Fitting Room	30531525
Enemy Controller	98045062
Energy Drain	56916805
Enervating Mist	26022485
Enraged Battle Ox	76909279
Eradicating Aerosol	94716515
Eternal Drought	56606928
Eternal Rest	95051344
Exarion Universe	63749102
Exchange	05556668
Exhausting Spell	95451366
Exodia Necross	12600382
Exodia the Forbidden One	33396948
Fairy Box	21598948
Fairy King Truesdale	45425051
Fairy Meteor Crush	97687912
Fairy's Hand Mirror	17653779
Fake Trap	03027001
Feather Shot	19394153
Feather Wind	71060915
Fengsheng Mirror	37406863
Feral Imp	41392891
Fiend Comedian	81172176
Fiend Skull Dragon	66235877

CARD	PASSWORD	CARD	PASSWORD
Fiend's Hand Mirror	58607704	Gokibore	15367030
Fiend's Sanctuary	24874630	Gorgon's Eye	52648457
Final Countdown	95308449	Graceful Dice	74137509
Final Destiny	18591904	Gradius' Option	14291024
Firewing Pegasus	27054370	Granadora	13944422
Fissure	66788016	Grand Tiki Elder	13676474
Flame Cerebrus	60862676	Gravedigger Ghoul	82542267
Flame Manipulator	34460851	Gravekeeper's Assailant	25262697
Flame Swordsman	40502030	Gravekeeper's Cannonholder	99877698
Flying Kamakiri #1	84834865	Gravekeeper's Chief	62473983
Foolish Burial	81439173	Gravekeeper's Commandant	17393207
Forced Ceasefire	97806240	Gravekeeper's Curse	50712728
Forest	87430998	Gravekeeper's Guard	37101832
Fortress Whale	62337487	Gravekeeper's Servant	16762927
Fortress Whale's Oath	77454922	Gravekeeper's Spear Soldier	63695531
Frozen Soul	57069605	Gravekeeper's Spy	24317029
Fulfillment of the Contract	48206762	Gravekeeper's Vassal	99690140
Full Salvo	70865988	Gravekeeper's Watcher	26084285
Fusilier Dragon, the Duel-Mode Beast	51632798	Gravity Axe - Grarl	32022366
Fusion Gate	24094653	Gravity Bind	85742772
Fusion Sage	26902560	Great Moth	14141448
Fusion Sword Murasame Blade	37684215	Greed	89405199
Gaia Power	56594520	Green Baboon, Defender of the Forest	46668237
Gaia the Dragon Champion	66889139	Greenkappa	61831093
Gaia the Fierce Knight	06368038	Ground Collapse	90502999
Gamma the Magnet Warrior	11549357	Gust	73079365
Garoozis	14977074	Gust Fan	55321970
Garuda the Wind Spirit	12800777	Gyaku-Gire Panda	09817927
Gazelle the King of Mythical Beasts	05818798	Hammer Shot	26412047
Gear Golem the Moving Fortress	30190809	Hand Collapse	74519184
Gearfried the Iron Knight	00423705	Hannibal Necromancer	05640330
Gearfried the Swordmaster	57046845	Harpie Lady	76812113
Gemini Elf	69140098	Harpie Lady 1	91932350
Generation Shift	34460239	Harpie Lady 2	27927359
Germ Infection	24668830	Harpie Lady 3	54415063
Getsu Fuhma	21887179	Harpie Lady Sisters	12206212
Giant Flea	41762634	Harpies' Hunting Ground	75782277
Giant Germ	95178994	Harpie's Pet Dragon	52040216
Giant Rat	97017120	Headless Knight	5434080
Giant Red Seasnake	58831685	Heart of Clear Water	64801562
Giant Soldier of Stone	13039848	Heart of the Underdog	35762283
Giant Trunade	42703248	Heavy Mech Support Platform	23265594
Gigantes	47606319	Heavy Slump	52417194
Gilasaurus	45894482	Heavy Storm	19613556
Gilford the Legend	69933858	Helpoemer	76052811
Gilford the Lightning	36354007	Hercules Beetle	52584282
Gil Garth	38445524	Hero Kid	32679370
Goblin Attack Force	78658564	Hero Signal	22020907
Goblin Fan	04149689	Hidden Book of Spell	21840375
Goblin King	18590133	Hieroglyph Lithograph	10248192
Goblin Thief	45311864	Hinotama	46130346
Goblin's Secret Remedy	11868825	Hiro's Shadow Scout	81863068
Goddess of Whim	67959180	Hitotsu-Me Giant	76184692
Goddess with the Third Eye	53493204	Horn Imp	69669405
		Horn of Light	38552107

CARD	PASSWORD	CARD	PASSWORD
Horn of the Unicorn	64047146	Left Leg of the Forbidden One	44519536
Hoshiningen	67629977	Legacy of Yata-Garasu	30461781
House of Adhesive Tape	15083728	Legendary Sword	61854111
Human-Wave Tactics	30353551	Level Conversion Lab	84397023
Illusionist Faceless Mage	28546905	Level Limit - Area A	54976796
Impenetrable Formation	96631852	Level Limit - Area B	03136426
Inferno	74823665	Level Modulation	61850482
Inferno Fire Blast	52684508	Level Up!	25290459
Infinite Cards	94163677	Light of Judgment	44595286
Infinite Dismissal	54109233	Lighten the Load	37231841
Injection Fairy Lily	79575620	Lightforce Sword	49587034
Insect Armor with Laser Cannon	03492538	Lightning Vortex	69162969
Insect Barrier	23615409	Little Chimera	68658728
Insect Imitation	96965364	Luminous Soldier	57482479
Insect Queen	91512835	Luminous Spark	81777047
Inspection	16227556	Luster Dragon	11091375
Interdimensional Matter Transporter	36261276	Machine Duplication	63995093
		Machine King	46700124
Invigoration	98374133	Mad Sword Beast	79870141
Jack's Knight	90876561	Mage Power	83746708
Jade Insect Whistle	95214051	Magic Cylinder	62279055
Jam Breeding Machine	21770260	Magic Drain	59344077
Jam Defender	21558682	Magic Formula	67227834
Jar of Greed	83968380	Magic Jammer	77414722
Jigen Bakudan	90020065	Magical Arm Shield	96008713
Jinzo	77585513	Magical Dimension	28553439
Jinzo #7	77585513	Magical Explosion	32723153
Jowgen the Spiritualist	41855169	Magical Hats	81210420
Jowls of Dark Demise	05257687	Magical Stone Excavation	98494543
Judge Man	30113682	Magical Thorn	53119267
Judgment of the Pharaoh	55948544	Magician of Black Chaos	30208479
Just Desserts	24068492	Magician of Faith	31560081
Kabazauls	51934376	Magician's Circle	00050755
Kabazauls	51934376	Magician's Unite	36045450
Kanan the Swordsmistress	12829151	Magician's Valkyria	80304126
Killer Needle	88979991	Maha Vailo	93013676
Kinetic Soldier	79853073	Maharaghi	40695128
King of the Skull Servants	36021814	Maiden of the Aqua	17214465
King of the Swamp	79109599	Major Riot	09074847
King Tiger Wanghu	83986578	Malevolent Catastrophe	01224927
King's Knight	64788463	Malevolent Nuzzler	99597615
Koitsu	69456283	Malfunction	06137091
Krokodilus	76512652	Malice Dispersion	13626450
Kryuel	82642348	Man-Eater Bug	54652250
Kunai with Chain	37390589	Man-Eating Treasure Chest	13723605
Kuriboh	40640057	Manga Ryu-Ran	38369349
Kycoo the Ghost Destroyer	88240808	Marauding Captain	02460565
Labyrinth of Nightmare	66526672	Marie the Fallen One	57579381
Labyrinth Tank	99551425	Marshmallon	31305911
Larvae Moth	87756343	Marshmallon Glasses	66865880
Laser Cannon Armor	77007920	Mask of Brutality	82432018
Last Day of the Witch	90330453	Mask of Darkness	28933734
Launcher Spider	87322377	Mask of Dispel	20765952
Lava Battleguard	20394040	Mask of Restrict	29549364
Lava Golem	00102380	Mask of the Accursed	56948373
Left Arm of the Forbidden One	07902349	Mask of Weakness	57882509

CARD	PASSWORD	CARD	PASSWORD
Masked Sorcerer	10189126	Mystical Elf	15025844
Mass Driver	34906152	Mystical Moon	36607978
Master Kyonshee	24530661	Mystical Refpanel	35563539
Mataza the Zapper	22609617	Mystical Sheep #1	30451366
Mausoleum of the Emperor	80921533	Mystical Space Typhoon	05318639
Mechanicalchaser	07359741	Narrow Pass	40172183
Mega Ton Magical Cannon	32062913	Necrovalley	47355498
Megamorph	22046459	Needle Wall	38299233
Melchid the Four-Faced Beast	86569121	Needle Worm	81843628
Meltiel, Sage of the Sky	49905576	Negate Attack	14315573
Mesmeric Control	48642904	Neo the Magic Swordsman	50930991
Messenger of Peace	44656491	Newdoria	04335645
Metal Detector	75646520	Next to be Lost	07076131
Metal Reflect Slime	26905245	Nightmare Wheel	54704216
Metalmorph	68540058	Nimble Momonga	22567609
Metalzoa	50705071	Nitro Unit	23842445
Meteor Black Dragon	90660762	Non Aggression Area	76848240
Meteor Dragon	64271667	Non-Fusion Area	27581098
Michizure	37580756	Non-Spellcasting Area	20065549
Micro Ray	18190572	Numinous Healer	02130625
Millennium Shield	32012841	Nuvia the Wicked	12953226
Milus Radiant	07489323	Obnoxious Celtic Guard	52077741
Mind Control	37520316	Ojama Black	79335209
Mind Crush	15800838	Ojama Delta Hurricane!!	08251996
Miracle Dig	63434080	Ojama Green	12482652
Miracle Kids	55985014	Ojama King	90140980
Miracle Restoring	68334074	Ojama Trio	29843091
Mirror Force	44095762	Ojama Yellow	42941100
Mispolymerization	58392024	Ojamagic	24643836
Mist body	47529357	Ojamuscle	98259197
Moisture Creature	75285069	Ominous Fortunetelling	56995655
Mokey Mokey	27288416	Ookazi	19523799
Mokey Mokey King	13803864	Opti-Camouflage Armor	44762290
Mokey Mokey Smackdown	01965724	Order to Charge	78986941
Molten Destruction	19384334	Order to Smash	39019325
Monster Gate	43040603	Otohime	39751093
Monster Recovery	93108433	Overpowering Eye	60577362
Monster Reincarnation	74848038	Panther Warrior	42035044
Mooyan Curry	58074572	Paralyzing Potion	50152549
Morphing Jar	33508719	Parasite Paracide	27911549
Morphing Jar #2	79106360	Parrot Dragon	62762898
Mother Grizzly	57839750	Patrician of Darkness	19153634
Mountain	50913601	Pendulum Machine	24433920
Muka Muka	46657337	Penguin Knight	36039163
Multiplication of Ants	22493811	Penguin Soldier	93920745
Multiply	40703222	Perfectly Ultimate Great Moth	48579379
Mushroom Man	14181608	Petit Moth	58192742
My Body as a Shield	69279219	Pharaoh's Treasure	63571750
Mysterious Puppeteer	54098121	Pigeonholing Books of Spell	96677818
Mystic Box	25774450	Pikeru's Second Sight	58015506
Mystic Horseman	68516705	Pinch Hopper	26185991
Mystic Probe	49251811	Pitch-Black Power Stone	34029630
Mystic Swordsman LV2	47507260	Poison Fangs	76539047
Mystic Swordsman LV4	74591968	Poison of the Old Man	08842266
Mystic Swordsman LV6	60482781	Polymerization	35550694
Mystic Tomato	83011277	Pot of Avarice	67169062

CARD	PASSWORD	CARD	PASSWORD
Premature Burial	70828912	Royal Surrender	56058888
Prepare to Strike Back	04483989	Royal Tribute	72405967
Prevent Rat	00549481	Rude Kaiser	26378150
Princess of Tsurugi	51371017	Rush Recklessly	70046172
Prohibition	43711255	Ryu Kokki	57281778
Protector of the Sanctuary	24221739	Ryu-Kishin	15303296
Pumpking the King of Ghosts	29155212	Ryu-Ran	02964201
Queen's Knight	25652259	Sage's Stone	13604200
Rabid Horseman	94905343	Saggi the Dark Clown	66602787
Radiant Jeral	84177693	Sakuretsu Armor	56120475
Radiant Mirror Force	21481146	Salamandra	32268901
Raigeki Break	04178474	Salvage	96947648
Rapid-Fire Magician	06337436	Sangan	26202165
Ray of Hope	82529174	Sasuke Samurai #3	77379481
Ready for Intercepting	31785398	Sasuke Samurai #4	64538655
Really Eternal Rest	28121403	Satellite Cannon	50400231
Reaper of the Cards	33066139	Second Coin Toss	36562627
Reckless Greed	37576645	Sengenjin	76232340
Recycle	96316857	Serial Spell	49398568
Red Archery Girl	65570596	Serpentine Princess	71829750
Red Medicine	38199696	Seven Tools of the Bandit	03819470
Red-Eyes B. Chick	36262024	Shadow Ghoul	30778711
Red-Eyes Black Dragon	74677422	Shadow of Eyes	58621589
Red-Eyes Black Metal Dragon	64335804	Share the Pain	56830749
Reflect Bounder	02851070	Shield & Sword	52097679
Reinforcement of the Army	32807846	Shield Crush	30683373
Reinforcements	17814387	Shift	59560625
Release Restraint	75417459	Shifting Shadows	59237154
Relieve Monster	37507488	Shinato, King of a Higher Plane	86327225
Relinquished	64631466	Shinato's Ark	60365591
Remove Trap	51482758	Shining Abyss	87303357
Respect Play	08951260	Shining Angel	95956346
Restructer Revolution	99518961	Shooting Star Bow - Ceal	95638658
Reversal Quiz	05990062	Shrink	55713623
Reverse Trap	77622396	Silver Bow and Arrow	01557499
Revival Jam	31709826	Simultaneous Loss	92219931
Right Arm of the Forbidden One	70903634	Skilled Dark Magician	73752131
Right Leg of the Forbidden One	08124921	Skilled White Magician	46363422
Rigorous Reaver	39180960	Skull Dice	00126218
Ring of Magnetism	20436034	Skull Servant	32274490
Riryoku Field	70344351	Skull-Mark Ladybug	64306248
Rising Energy	78211862	Skyscraper	63035430
Rite of Spirit	30450531	Slate Warrior	78636495
Ritual Weapon	54351224	Slot Machine	03797883
Robbin' Goblin	88279736	Smashing Ground	97169186
Robbin' Zombie	83258273	Smoke Grenade of the Thief	63789924
Robotic Knight	44203504	Snake Fang	00596051
Rock Bombardment	20781762	Sogen	86318356
Rocket Warrior	30860696	Solar Ray	44472639
Rod of Silence - Kay'est	95515060	Solemn Judgment	41420027
Rogue Doll	91939608	Solemn Wishes	35346968
Roll Out!	91597389	Sorcerer of the Doomed	49218300
Royal Command	33950246	Soul Absorption	68073522
Royal Decree	51452091	Soul Demolition	76297408
Royal Magical Library	70791313	Soul Exchange	68005187
Royal Oppression	93016201	Soul of Purity and Light	77527210

CARD	PASSWORD
Soul of the Pure	47852924
Soul Release	05758500
Soul Resurrection	92924317
Soul Reversal	78864369
Soul Taker	81510157
Spark Blaster	97362768
Spatial Collapse	20644748
Special Hurricane	42598242
Spell Absorption	51481927
Spell Reproduction	29228529
Spell Vanishing	29735721
Spellbinding Circle	18807108
Spell-stopping Statute	10069186
Spiral Spear Strike	49328340
Spirit Message "A"	94772232
Spirit Message "I"	31893528
Spirit Message "L"	30170981
Spirit Message "N"	67287533
Spirit of Flames	13522325
Spirit of the Pharaoh	25343280
Spirit's Invitation	92394653
Spiritual Earth Art - Kurogane	70156997
Spiritual Energy Settle Machine	99173029
Spiritual Fire Art - Kurenai	42945701
Spiritual Water Art - Aoi	06540606
Spiritual Wind Art - Miyabi	79333300
Spiritualism	15866454
St. Joan	21175632
Staunch Defender	92854392
Steel Ogre Grotto #2	90908427
Steel Scorpion	13599884
Stim-Pack	83225447
Stone Statue of the Aztecs	31812496
Stop Defense	63102017
Stray Lambs	60764581
Stumbling	34646691
Swamp Battleguard	40453765
Swift Gaia the Fierce Knight	16589042
Sword of Deep-Seated	98495314
Sword of the Soul-Eater	05371656
Swords of Concealing Light	12923641
Swords of Revealing Light	72302403
Swordsman of Landstar	03573512
System Down	07672244
Tailor of the Fickle	43641473
Terraforming	73628505
The A. Forces	00403847
The Agent of Force - Mars	91123920
The Agent of Judgement - Saturn	91345518
The Big March of Animals	01689516
The Bistro Butcher	71107816
The Cheerful Coffin	41142615
The Creator	61505339
The Creator Incarnate	97093037
The Dark Door	30606547
The Earl of Demise	66989694

CARD	PASSWORD
The Fiend Megacyber	66362965
The First Sarcophagus	31076103
The Flute of Summoning Kuriboh	20065322
The Forgiving Maiden	84080938
The Gross Ghost of Fled Dreams	68049471
The Illusory Gentleman	83764996
The Inexperienced Spy	81820689
The Last Warrior from Another Planet	86099788
The Law of the Normal	66926224
The League of Uniform Nomenclature	55008284
The Little Swordsman of Aile	25109950
The Masked Beast	49064413
The Portrait's Secret	32541773
The Regulation of Tribe	00296499
The Reliable Guardian	16430187
The Rock Spirit	76305638
The Sanctuary in the Sky	56433456
The Second Sarcophagus	04081094
The Secret of the Bandit	99351431
The Shallow Grave	43434803
The Snake Hair	29491031
The Spell Absorbing Life	99517131
The Statue of Easter Island	10261698
The Third Sarcophagus	78697395
The Unhappy Girl	27618634
The Unhappy Maiden	51275027
The Warrior Returning Alive	95281259
The Wicked Worm Beast	06285791
Thestalos the Firestorm Monarch	26205777
Thousand Dragon	41462083
Thousand Energy	05703682
Thousand Knives	63391643
Thousand-Eyes Idol	27125110
Threatening Roar	36361633
Three-Headed Geedo	78423643
Thunder Crash	69196160
Thunder Dragon	31786629
Thunder Nyan Nyan	70797118
Time Machine	80987696
Time Wizard	06285791
Token Feastevil	83675475
Toon Alligator	59383041
Toon Cannon Soldier	79875176
Toon Dark Magician Girl	90960358
Toon Defense	43509019
Toon Gemini Elf	42386471
Toon Goblin Attack Force	15270885
Toon Masked Sorcerer	16392422
Toon Mermaid	65458948
Toon Summoned Skull	91842653
Toon Table of Contents	89997728
Toon World	15259703
Tornado	61068510
Tornado Wall	18605135

CARD	PASSWORD	CARD	PASSWORD
Torpedo Fish	90337190	Waboku	12607053
Tower of Babel	94256039	Wall of Illusion	13945283
Tragedy	35686187	Wall of Revealing Light	17078030
Transcendent Wings	25573054	Wall Shadow	63162310
Trap Hole	04206964	Warrior Elimination	90873992
Trap Jammer	19252988	Warrior Lady of the Wasteland	05438492
Trap Master	46461247	Wasteland	98239899
Tremendous Fire	46918794	Weapon Change	10035717
Triage	30888983	Weather Report	72053645
Triangle Ecstasy Spark	12181376	Weed Out	28604635
Triangle Power	32298781	White Magical Hat	15150365
Tribute Doll	02903036	White-Horned Dragon	73891874
Tribute to the Doomed	79759861	Wicked-Breaking Flamberge - Baou	68427465
Tri-Horned Dragon	39111158	Widespread Ruin	77754944
Twin Swords of Flashing Light - Tryce	21900719	Wild Nature's Release	61166988
Twin-Headed Behemoth	43586926	Winged Dragon, Guardian of the Fortress #1	87796900
Twin-Headed Thunder Dragon	54752875	Winged Kuriboh	57116033
Two-Headed King Rex	94119974	Winged Kuriboh LV10	98585345
Two-Pronged Attack	83887306	Witch's Apprentice	80741828
Tyhone	72842870	Wolf	49417509
Type Zero Magic Crusher	35346968	Wolf Axwielder	56369281
UFO Turtle	60806437	Woodland Sprite	06979239
Ultimate Offering	80604091	World Suppression	12253117
Ultra Evolution Pill	22431243	Xing Zhen Hu	76515293
Umiiruka	82999629	Yamata Dragon	76862289
Union Attack	60399954	Yami	59197169
United We Stand	56747793	Yellow Luster Shield	04542651
Unity	14731897	Yu-Jo Friendship	81332143
Upstart Goblin	70368879	Zaborg the Thunder Monarch	51945556
Uraby	01784619	Zero Gravity	83133491
Valkyrion the Magna Warrior	75347539	Zoa	24311372
Versago the Destroyer	50259460	Zolga	16268841
Vile Germs	39774685	Zombie Warrior	31339260
Vorse Raider	14898066		

YU-GI-OH! WORLD CHAMPIONSHIP 2007

CARD PASSWORDS

Select Password from the Shop and enter one of the Card Passwords. You must already have that card or have it in a pack list for the password to work. Refer to the Card List for YU-GI-OH! GX TAG FORCE for PSP. All cards may not be available in World Championship 2007.

ZOO KEEPER

GEKIMUZU DIFFICULTY

Earn a high score in all 4 modes.
Here are the high scores needed for each mode:

MODE	SCORE
Zoo keeper	200000
Tokoton 100	800000
Quest mode	10000
Time attack	600000

ZOO TYCOON DS

UNLOCK EVERYTHING

At the Main menu, press Up, Up, Down, Down, Left, Right, Left, Right, Up, Up, Down , Down, Left, Right, Left, Right.

PLAYSTATION® PORTABLE

CONTENTS

PLAYSTATIO

ATV OFFROAD FURY: BLAZIN' TRAILS

UNLOCK EVERYTHING EXCEPT THE FURY BIKE

Select Player Profile from Options. Choose Enter Cheat and enter All Access.

1500 CREDITS

Select Player Profile from Options. Choose Enter Cheat and enter $moneybags$.

ALL RIDER GEAR

Select Player Profile from Options. Choose Enter Cheat and enter Duds.

MUSIC VIDEOS

Select Player Profile from Options. Choose Enter Cheat and enter Billboards.

TIRES

Select Player Profile from Options. Choose Enter Cheat and enter Dubs.

BEN 10: ALIEN FORCE THE GAME

LEVEL LORD

Enter Gwen, Kevin, Big Chill, Gwen as a code.

INVINCIBILITY

Enter Kevin, Big Chill, Swampfire, Kevin as a code.

ALL COMBOS

Enter Swampfire, Gwen, Kevin, Ben as a code.

INFINITE ALIENS

Enter Ben, Swampfire, Gwen, Big Chill as a code.

BEN 10: PROTECTOR OF EARTH

INVINCIBILITY

Select a game from the Continue option. Go to the Map Selection screen, press Start and choose Extras. Select Enter Secret Code and enter XLR8, Heatblast, Wildvine, Fourarms.

ALL COMBOS

Select a game from the Continue option. Go to the Map Selection screen, press Start and choose Extras. Select Enter Secret Code and enter Cannonblot, Heatblast, Fourarms, Heatblast.

ALL LOCATIONS

Select a game from the Continue option. Go to the Map Selection screen, press Start and choose Extras. Select Enter Secret Code and enter Heatblast, XLR8, XLR8, Cannonblot.

DNA FORCE SKINS

Select a game from the Continue option. Go to the Map Selection screen, press Start and choose Extras. Select Enter Secret Code and enter Wildvine, Fourarms, Heatblast, Cannonbolt.

DARK HEROES SKINS

Select a game from the Continue option. Go to the Map Selection screen, press Start and choose Extras. Select Enter Secret Code and enter Cannonbolt, Cannonbolt, Fourarms, Heatblast.

ALL ALIEN FORMS

Select a game from the Continue option. Go to the Map Selection screen, press Start and choose Extras. Select Enter Secret Code and enter Wildvine, Fourarms, Heatblast, Wildvine.

MASTER CONTROL

Select a game from the Continue option. Go to the Map Selection screen, press Start and choose Extras. Select Enter Secret Code and enter Cannonbolt, Heatblast, Wildvine, Fourarms.

BURNOUT LEGENDS

COP RACER

Earn a Gold in all Pursuit events.

FIRE TRUCK

Earn a Gold on all Crash Events.

GANGSTER BOSS

Earn Gold in all Race events.

CAPCOM CLASSICS COLLECTION REMIXED

UNLOCK EVERYTHING

At the title screen, press Left on D-pad, Right on D-pad, Left on Analog stick, Right on Analog stick, ●, ●, Up on D-pad, Down on D-pad.

CAPCOM PUZZLE WORLD

SUPER BUSTER BROS.

LEVEL SELECT IN TOUR MODE

At the Main menu, highlight Tour Mode, hold Down and press ❌.

SUPER PUZZLE FIGHTER

PLAY AS AKUMA

At the character select, highlight Hsien-Ko and press Down.

PLAY AS DAN

At the character select, highlight Donovan and press Down.

PLAY AS DEVILOT

At the character select, highlight Morrigan and press Down.

PLAY AS ANITA

At the character select, hold L + R and choose Donovan.

PLAY AS HSIEN-KO'S TALISMAN

At the character select, hold L + R and choose Hsien-Ko.

PLAY AS MORRIGAN AS A BAT

At the character select, hold L + R and choose Morrigan.

CARS

BONUS SPEEDWAY (REVERSED) IN CUSTOM RACE

At the Main menu hold L and press ❌, ⬛, ▲, ❌, ▲, ⬛.

Bonus
Speedway (Reversed)

ALL CARS, PAINTJOBS, TRACKS, MOVIE CLIPS AND MODES

At the main menu, hold L and press ▲, ⬛, ❌, ⬤, ▲, ❌, ⬛, ▲, ⬤, ❌.

UNLIMITED NITROUS

At the main menu, hold L and ❌, ⬛, ⬤, ⬤, ⬤, ▲, ⬛, ❌.

CASTLEVANIA: THE DRACULA X CHRONICLES

SYMPHONY OF THE NIGHT

After clearing the game as Alucard, select New Game and enter the following as your name:

PLAY AS ALUCARD, WITH 99 LUCK AND THE LAPIS LAZULI

X-X!V''Q

PLAY AS ALUCARD, WITH THE AXE LORD ARMOR

AXEARMOR

PLAY AS MARIA RENARD

MARIA

PLAY AS RICHTER BELMONT

RICHTER

CRISIS CORE—FINAL FANTASY VII

NEW GAME+

After completing the game, you'll be prompted to make a new save. Loading a game from this new save will begin a New Game+, starting the game over while allowing Zack to retain almost everything he's earned.

The following items transfer to a New Game+:

Level, Experience, SP, Gil, Playtime, Non-Key Items, Materia, and DMW Completion Rate

The following items do not transfer:

Key Items, Materia/Accessory Slot Expansion, Ability to SP Convert, DMW Images, Mission Progress, Mail, and Unlocked Shops

EXIT

SITUATION 8

Complete Situation 1. Then at the Title screen, press L, R, Left, Right, ●, ◎, ✖, ▲.

SITUATION 9

Complete Situation 1 and unlock Situation 8. Then at the Title screen, press ▲, Down, ◎, Left, ✖, Up, ●, Right.

SITUATION 10

Complete Situation 1 and unlock Situations 8 and 9. Then at the Title screen, press Right, Down, Up, Left, ◎, ✖, R, L.

FINAL FANTASY TACTICS: THE WAR OF THE LIONS

MUSIC TEST MODE

Enter the main character's name as PolkaPolka at the name entry screen.

FLATOUT: HEAD ON

1 MILLION CREDITS

Select Enter Code from the Extras menu and enter GIVECASH.

ALL CARS AND 1 MILLION CREDITS

Select Enter Code from the Extras menu and enter GIEVEPIX.

BIG RIG

Select Enter Code from the Extras menu and enter ELPUEBLO.

BIG RIG TRUCK

Select Enter Code from the Extras menu and enter RAIDERS.

FLATMOBILE CAR

Select Enter Code from the Extras menu and enter WOTKINS.

MOB CAR

Select Enter Code from the Extras menu and enter BIGTRUCK.

PIMPSTER CAR

Select Enter Code from the Extras menu and enter RUTTO.

ROCKET CAR

Select Enter Code from the Extras menu and enter KALJAKOPPA.

SCHOOL BUS

Select Enter Code from the Extras menu and enter GIEVCARPLZ.

FULL AUTO 2: BATTLELINES

ALL CARS

Select Cheats from the Options and press Up, Up, Up, Up, Left, Down, Up, Right, Down, Down, Down, Down.

ALL EVENTS

Select Cheats from the Options and press Start, Left, Select, Right, Right, ▲, ✖, ●, Start, R, Down, Select.

GRADIUS COLLECTION

ALL WEAPONS & POWER-UPS ON EASY DIFFICULTY

Pause the game and press Up, Up, Down, Down, Left, Right, Left, Right, ✖, ●.

GRADIUS COLLECTION

ALL WEAPONS & POWER-UPS

Pause the game and press Up, Up, Down, Down, Left, Right, Left, Right, L, R. This code can be used once per level.

HOT BRAIN

119.99 TEMPERATURE IN ALL 5 CATEGORIES

Select New Game and enter Cheat.

HOT SHOTS GOLF 2

UNLOCK EVERYTHING

Enter 2gsh as your name.

IRON MAN

Iron Man's different armor suits are unlocked by completing certain missions.

COMPLETE MISSION	SUIT UNLOCKED
1, Escape	Mark I
2, First Flight	Mark II
3, Fight Back	Mark III
5, Maggia Compound	Gold Tin Can
8, Frozen Ship	Classic
11, Island Meltdown	Stealth
13, Showdown	Titanium Man

PSP MINIGAMES

Minigames can be unlocked by completing the following missions. Access the minigames through the Bonus menu.

COMPLETE MISSION	PSP MINIGAME UNLOCKED
1, Escape	Tin Can Challenge 1 + 2
2, First Flight	DEATH RACE: STARK INDUSTRY
3, Fight Back	BOSS FIGHT: DREADNOUGHT
4, Weapons Transport	DEATH RACE: AFGHAN DESERT
	BOSS FIGHT: WHIPLASH
5, Maggia Compound	DEATH RACE: MAGGIA MANSION
6, Flying Fortress	SPEED KILL: FLYING FORTRESS
	SURVIVAL: FLYING FORTRESS
7, Nuclear Winter	DEATH RACE: ARTIC CIRCLE

COMPLETE MISSION	PSP MINIGAME UNLOCKED
8, Frozen Ship	SPEED KILL: FROZEN SHIP
	SURVIVAL: FROZEN SHIP
9, Home Front	BOSS FIGHT: TITANIUM MAN
10, Save Pepper	DEATH RACE: DAM BASSIN
11, Island Meltdown	SPEED KILL: GREEK ISLANDS
	SURVIVAL: GREEK ISLANDS
12, Battlesuit Factory	SPEED KILL: TINMEN FACTORY
	SURVIVAL: TINMEN FACTORY
13, Showdown	BOSS FIGHT: IRON MONGER

CONCEPT ART

As you progress through the game and destroy the Weapon Crates, bonuses are unlocked. You can find all of these in the Bonus menu once unlocked.

CONCEPT ART UNLOCKED	NUMBER OF WEAPON CRATES FOUND
Environments Set 1	6
Environments Set 2	12
Iron Man	18
Environments Set 3	24
Enemies	30
Environments Set 4	36
Villains	42
Vehicles	48
Covers	50

JUICED: ELIMINATOR

ALL CARS AND TRACKS IN ARCADE MODE

Select Cheats from the Extras menu and enter PIES.

UNLOCK EVERYTHING

Pause the game, hold L + R and press Down, Left, Up, Right.

INVINCIBLE

Pause the game, hold L + R and press Left, Down, Right, Up, Left, Down, Right, Up.

UNLIMITED ENERGY

Pause the game, hold L + R and press Down, Down, Right, Right, Up, Up, Left, Left.

LAST MAN STANDING CHALLENGE AND AN ASCARI KZ1

Select Cheats and Challenges from the DNA Lab menu and enter KNOX. Defeat the challenge to earn the Ascari KZ1.

SPECIAL CHALLENGE AND AN AUDI TT 1.8 QUATTRO

Select Cheats and Challenges from the DNA Lab menu and enter YTHZ. Defeat the challenge to earn the Audi TT 1.8 Quattro.

SPECIAL CHALLENGE AND A BMW Z4

Select Cheats and Challenges from the DNA Lab menu and enter GVDL. Defeat the challenge to earn the BMW Z4.

SPECIAL CHALLENGE AND A HOLDEN MONARO

Select Cheats and Challenges from the DNA Lab menu and enter RBSG. Defeat the challenge to earn the Holden Monaro.

SPECIAL CHALLENGE AND A HYUNDAI COUPE 2.7 V6

Select Cheats and Challenges from the DNA Lab menu and enter BSLU. Defeat the challenge to earn the Hyundai Coupe 2.7 V6.

SPECIAL CHALLENGE AND AN INFINITY G35

Select Cheats and Challenges from the DNA Lab menu and enter MRHC. Defeat the challenge to earn the Infinity G35.

SPECIAL CHALLENGE AND AN INFINITY RED G35

Select Cheats and Challenges from the DNA Lab menu and enter MNCH. Defeat the challenge to earn the Infinity G35.

SPECIAL CHALLENGE AND A KOENIGSEGG CCX

Select Cheats and Challenges from the DNA Lab menu and enter KDTR. Defeat the challenge to earn the Koenigsegg CCX.

SPECIAL CHALLENGE AND A MITSUBISHI PROTOTYPE X

Select Cheats and Challenges from the DNA Lab menu and enter DOPX. Defeat the challenge to earn the Mitsubishi Prototype X.

SPECIAL CHALLENGE AND A NISSAN 350Z

Select Cheats and Challenges from the DNA Lab menu and enter PRGN. Defeat the challenge to earn the Nissan 350Z.

SPECIAL CHALLENGE AND A NISSAN SKYLINE R34 GT-R

Select Cheats and Challenges from the DNA Lab menu and enter JWRS. Defeat the challenge to earn the Nissan Skyline R34 GT-R.

SPECIAL CHALLENGE AND A SALEEN S7

Select Cheats and Challenges from the DNA Lab menu and enter WIKF. Defeat the challenge to earn the Saleen S7.

SPECIAL CHALLENGE AND A SEAT LEON CUPRA R

Select Cheats and Challenges from the DNA Lab menu and enter FAMQ. Defeat the challenge to earn the Seat Leon Cupra R.

BATCAVE CODES

Using the computer in the Batcave, select Enter Code and enter the following codes.

CHARACTERS

CHARACTER	CODE	CHARACTER	CODE
Alfred	ZAQ637	Penguin Henchman	BJH782
Batgirl	JKR331	Penguin Minion	KJP748
Bruce Wayne	BDJ327	Poison Ivy Goon	GTB899
Catwoman (Classic)	M1AAWW	Police Marksman	HKG984
Clown Goon	HJK327	Police Officer	JRY983
Commissioner Gordon	DDP967	Riddler Goon	CRY928
Fishmonger	HGY748	Riddler Henchman	XEU824
Freeze Girl	XVK541	S.W.A.T.	HTF114
Joker Goon	UTF782	Sailor	NAV592
Joker Henchman	YUN924	Scientist	JFL786
Mad Hatter	JCA283	Security Guard	PLB946
Man-Bat	NYU942	The Joker (Tropical)	CCB199
Military Policeman	MKL382	Yeti	NJL412
Nightwing	MVY759	Zoo Sweeper	DWR243
Penguin Goon	NKA238		

VEHICLES

VEHICLE	CODE	VEHICLE	CODE
Bat-Tank	KNTT4B	Mr. Freeze's Kart	BCT229
Bruce Wayne's Private Jet	LEA664	Penguin Goon Submarine	BTN248
Catwoman's Motorcycle	HPL826	Police Bike	LJP234
Garbage Truck	DUS483	Police Boat	PLC999
Goon Helicopter	GCH328	Police Car	KJL832
Harbor Helicopter	CHP735	Police Helicopter	CWR732
Harley Quinn's Hammer Truck	RDT637	Police Van	MAC788
Mad Hatter's Glider	HS000W	Police Watercraft	VJD328
Mad Hatter's Steamboat	M4DM4N	Riddler's Jet	HAHAHA
Mr. Freeze's Iceberg	ICYICE	Robin's Submarine	TTF453
The Joker's Van	JUK657	Two-Face's Armored Truck	EFE933

CHEATS

CHEAT	CODE	CHEAT	CODE
Always Score Multiply	9LRGNB	More Batarang Targets	XWP645
Fast Batarangs	JRBDCB	Piece Detector	KHJ554
Fast Walk	ZOLM6N	Power Brick Detector	MMN786
Flame Batarang	D8NYWH	Regenerate Hearts	HJH7HJ
Freeze Batarang	XPN4NG	Score x2	N4NR3E
Extra Hearts	ML3KHP	Score x4	CX9MAT
Fast Build	EVG26J	Score x6	MLVNF2
Immune to Freeze	JXUDY6	Score x8	WCCDB9
Invincibility	WYD5CP	Score x10	18HW07
Minikit Detector	ZXGH9J		

LEGO INDIANA JONES: THE ORIGINAL ADVENTURES

CHARACTERS

Approach the blackboard in the Classsroom and enter the following codes.

CHARACTER	CODE	CHARACTER	CODE
Bandit	12N68W	Fedora	V75YSP
Bandit Swordsman	1MK4RT	First Mate	0GIN24
Barranca	04EM94	Grail Knight	NE6THI
Bazooka Trooper (Crusade)	MK83R7	Hovitos Tribesman	HOV1SS
Bazooka Trooper (Raiders)	S93Y5R	Indiana Jones (Desert Disguise)	4J8S4M
Belloq	CHN3YU	Indiana Jones (Officer)	VJ850S
Belloq (Jungle)	TDR197	Jungle Guide	24PF34
Belloq (Robes)	VEO29L	Kao Kan	WMO46L
British Commander	B73EUA	Kazim	NRH23J
British Officer	VJ5TI9	Kazim (Desert)	3M29TJ
British Soldier	DJ5I2W	Lao Che	2NK479
Captain Katanga	VJ3TT3	Maharajah	NFK5N2
Chatter Lal	ENW936	Major Toht	13NS01
Chatter Lal (Thuggee)	CNH4RY	Masked Bandit	N48SF0
Chen	3NK48T	Mola Ram	FJUR31
Colonel Dietrich	2K9RKS	Monkey Man	3RF6YJ
Colonel Vogel	8EAL4H	Pankot Assassin	2NKT72
Dancing Girl	C7EJ21	Pankot Guard	VN28RH
Donovan	3NFTU8	Sherpa Brawler	VJ37WJ
Elsa (Desert)	JSNRT9	Sherpa Gunner	ND762W
Elsa (Officer)	VMJ5US	Slave Child	0E3ENW
Enemy Boxer	8246RB	Thuggee	VM683E
Enemy Butler	VJ48W3	Thuggee Acolyte	T2R3F9
Enemy Guard	VJ7R51	Thuggee Slave Driver	VBS7GW
Enemy Guard (Mountains)	YR47WM	Village Dignitary	KD48TN
Enemy Officer	572E61	Village Elder	4682E1
Enemy Officer (Desert)	2MK450	Willie (Dinner Suit)	VK93R7
Enemy Pilot	B84ELP	Willie (Pajamas)	MEN4IP
Enemy Radio Operator	1MF94R	Wu Han	3NSLT8
Enemy Soldier (Desert)	4NSU7Q		

EXTRAS

Approach the blackboard in the Classsroom and enter the following codes. Some cheats need to be enabled by selecting Extras from the pause menu.

CHEAT	CODE	CHEAT	CODE
Artifact Detector	VIKED7	Regenerate Hearts	MDLP69
Beep Beep	VNF59Q	Secret Characters	3X44AA
Character Treasure	VIES2R	Silhouettes	3HE85H
Disarm Enemies	VKRNS9	Super Scream	VN3R7S
Disguises	4ID1N6	Super Slap	0P1TA5
Fast Build	V83SL0	Treasure Magnet	H86LA2
Fast Dig	378RS6	Treasure x10	VI3PS8
Fast Fix	FJ59WS	Treasure x2	VM4TS9
Fertilizer	B1GW1F	Treasure x4	VLWEN3
Ice Rink	33GM7J	Treasure x6	V84RYS
Parcel Detector	VUT673	Treasure x8	A72E1M
Poo Treasure	WWQ1SA		

LEGO STAR WARS II: THE ORIGINAL TRILOGY

BEACH TROOPER

At Mos Eisley Canteena, select Enter Code and enter UCK868. You still need to select
Characters and purchase this character for 20,000 studs.

BEN KENOBI (GHOST)

At Mos Eisley Canteena, select Enter Code and enter BEN917. You still need to select
Characters and purchase this character for 1,100,000 studs.

BESPIN GUARD

At Mos Eisley Canteena, select Enter Code and enter VHY832. You still need to select
Characters and purchase this character for 15,000 studs.

BIB FORTUNA

At Mos Eisley Canteena, select Enter Code and enter WTY721. You still need to select
Characters and purchase this character for 16,000 studs.

BOBA FETT

At Mos Eisley Canteena, select Enter Code and enter HLP221. You still need to select
Characters and purchase this character for 175,000 studs.

DEATH STAR TROOPER

At Mos Eisley Canteena, select Enter Code and enter BNC332. You still need to select
Characters and purchase this character for 19,000 studs.

EWOK

At Mos Eisley Canteena, select Enter Code and enter TTT289. You still need to select Characters
and purchase this character for 34,000 studs.

GAMORREAN GUARD

At Mos Eisley Canteena, select Enter Code and enter YZF999. You still need to select
Characters and purchase this character for 40,000 studs.

GONK DROID

At Mos Eisley Canteena, select Enter Code and enter NFX582. You still need to select
Characters and purchase this character for 1,550 studs.

GRAND MOFF TARKIN

At Mos Eisley Canteena, select Enter Code and enter SMG219. You still need to select
Characters and purchase this character for 38,000 studs.

GREEDO

At Mos Eisley Canteena, select Enter Code and enter NAH118. You still need to select Characters and purchase this character for 60,000 studs.

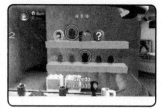

HAN SOLO (HOOD)

At Mos Eisley Canteena, select Enter Code and enter YWM840. You still need to select Characters and purchase this character for 20,000 studs.

IG-88

At Mos Eisley Canteena, select Enter Code and enter NXL973. You still need to select Characters and purchase this character for 30,000 studs.

IMPERIAL GUARD

At Mos Eisley Canteena, select Enter Code and enter MMM111. You still need to select Characters and purchase this character for 45,000 studs.

IMPERIAL OFFICER

At Mos Eisley Canteena, select Enter Code and enter BBV889. You still need to select Characters and purchase this character for 28,000 studs.

IMPERIAL SHUTTLE PILOT

At Mos Eisley Canteena, select Enter Code and enter VAP664. You still need to select Characters and purchase this character for 29,000 studs.

IMPERIAL SPY

At Mos Eisley Canteena, select Enter Code and enter CVT125. You still need to select Characters and purchase this character for 13,500 studs.

JAWA

At Mos Eisley Canteena, select Enter Code and enter JAW499. You still need to select Characters and purchase this character for 24,000 studs.

LOBOT

At Mos Eisley Canteena, select Enter Code and enter UUB319. You still need to select Characters and purchase this character for 11,000 studs.

PALACE GUARD

At Mos Eisley Canteena, select Enter Code and enter SGE549. You still need to select Characters and purchase this character for 14,000 studs.

REBEL PILOT

At Mos Eisley Canteena, select Enter Code and enter CYG336. You still need to select Characters and purchase this character for 15,000 studs.

REBEL TROOPER (HOTH)

At Mos Eisley Canteena, select Enter Code and enter EKU849. You still need to select Characters and purchase this character for 16,000 studs.

SANDTROOPER

At Mos Eisley Canteena, select Enter Code and enter YDV451. You still need to select Characters and purchase this character for 14,000 studs.

SKIFF GUARD

At Mos Eisley Canteena, select Enter Code and enter GBU888. You still need to select Characters and purchase this character for 12,000 studs.

SNOWTROOPER

At Mos Eisley Canteena, select Enter Code and enter NYU989. You still need to select Characters and purchase this character for 16,000 studs.

STROMTROOPER

At Mos Eisley Canteena, select Enter Code and enter PTR345. You still need to select Characters and purchase this character for 10,000 studs.

THE EMPEROR

At Mos Eisley Canteena, select Enter Code and enter HHY382. You still need to select Characters and purchase this character for 275,000 studs.

TIE FIGHTER

At Mos Eisley Canteena, select Enter Code and enter HDY739. You still need to select Characters and purchase this character for 60,000 studs.

TIE FIGHTER PILOT

At Mos Eisley Canteena, select Enter Code and enter NNZ316. You still need to select Characters and purchase this character for 21,000 studs.

TIE INTERCEPTOR

At Mos Eisley Canteena, select Enter Code and enter QYA828. You still need to select Characters and purchase this character for 40,000 studs.

TUSKEN RAIDER

At Mos Eisley Canteena, select Enter Code and enter PEJ821. You still need to select Characters and purchase this character for 23,000 studs.

UGNAUGHT

At Mos Eisley Canteena, select Enter Code and enter UGN694. You still need to select Characters and purchase this character for 36,000 studs.

MAJOR LEAGUE BASEBALL 2K7

MICKEY MANTLE ON THE FREE AGENTS LIST

Select Enter Cheat Code from the My 2K7 menu and enter themick.

MICKEY PINCH HITS

Select Enter Cheat Code from the My 2K7 menu and enter phmantle.

UNLOCK EVERYTHING

Select Enter Cheat Code from the My 2K7 menu and enter Derek Jeter. This does not unlock the Topps cheats.

ALL CHEATS

Select Enter Cheat Code from the My 2K7 menu and enter Black Sox.

ALL EXTRAS
Select Enter Cheat Code from the My 2K7 menu and enter Game On.

MIGHTY MICK CHEAT
Select Enter Cheat Code from the My 2K7 menu and enter mightymick.

TRIPLE CROWN CHEAT
Select Enter Cheat Code from the My 2K7 menu and enter triplecrown.

BIG BLAST CHEAT
Select Enter Cheat Code from the My 2K7 menu and enter m4murder.

MARVEL ULTIMATE ALLIANCE

UNLOCK ALL SKINS
At the Team menu, press Up, Down, Left, Right, Left, Right, Start.

UNLOCKS ALL HERO POWERS
At the Team menu, press Left, Right, Up, Down, Up, Down, Start.

ALL HEROES TO LEVEL 99
At the Team menu, press Up, Left, Up, Left, Down, Right, Down, Right, Start.

UNLOCK ALL HEROES
At the Team menu, press Up, Up, Down, Down, Left, Left, Left, Start.

UNLOCK DAREDEVIL
At the Team menu, press Left, Left, Right, Right, Up, Down, Up, Down, Start.

UNLOCK SILVER SURFER
At the Team menu, press Down, Left, Left, Up, Right, Up, Down, Left, Start.

GOD MODE
During gameplay, press Up, Down, Up, Down, Up, Left, Down, Right, Start.

TOUCH OF DEATH
During gameplay, press Left, Right, Down, Down, Right, Left, Start.

SUPER SPEED
During gameplay, press Up, Left, Up, Right, Down, Right, Start.

FILL MOMENTUM
During gameplay, press Left, Right, Right, Left, Up, Down, Down, Up, Start.

UNLOCK ALL COMICS
At the Review menu, press Left, Right, Right, Left, Up, Up, Right, Start.

UNLOCK ALL CONCEPT ART
At the Review menu, press Down, Down, Down, Right, Right, Left, Down, Start.

UNLOCK ALL CINEMATICS
At the Review menu, press Up, Left, Left, Up, Right, Right, Up, Start.

UNLOCK ALL LOAD SCREENS
At the Review menu, press Up, Down, Right, Left, Up, Up Down, Start.

UNLOCK ALL COURSES
At the Comic Missions menu, press Up, Right, Left, Down, Up, Right, Left, Down, Start.

PLAYSTATION® PORTABLE

CHEAT CODE EXPLOSION FOR HANDHELDS

METAL GEAR SOLID: PORTABLE OPS PLUS

SOLDIER PASSWORDS

Enter the following as a password.

SOLDIER	PASSWORD
Alabama	BB6K768KM9
Alaska	XL5SW5NH9S
Arizona	ZHEFPVV947
Arkansas	VNRE7JNQ8WE
Black Genome	WYNGG3JBP3YS
Blue Genome	9GNPHGFFLH
California	6MSJQYWNCJ8
Colorado	W6TAH498DJ
Connecticut	2N2AB3JV2WA
Delaware	AJRL6E7TT9
Female Scientist 1	3W8WVRGB2LNN
Female Scientist 2	FUC72C463KZ
Female Scientist 3	UCAWYTMXB5V
Female Soldier 1	UZZQYRPXM86
Female Soldier 2	QRQQ7GWKHJ
Female Soldier 3	MVNDAZAP8DWE
Florida	A44STZ3BHY5
Fox Soldier 1	FMXT79TPV4U8
Fox Soldier 2	HGMK3WCYURM
Fox Soldier 3	6ZY5NYW4TGK
Georgia	VD5H53JJCRH
Green Genome	TGQ6F5TUHD
GRU Soldier	9V8S7DVYFTR
Gurlukovich's Soldier	6VWM6A22FSS8
Hawaii	TW7ZMZHCBL
Hideochan Soldier	RU8XRCLPUUT
High Official	ADPS2SE5UC8
High Rank Officer 1	DVB2UDTQ5Z
High Rank Officer 2	84ZEC4X5PJ6
High Ranking Officer 3	DTAZ3QRQQDU
High-Tech Soldier	M4MSJ6R87XPP
Idaho	XAFGETZGXHGA
Illinois	QYUVCNDFUPZJ
Indiana	L68JVXVBL8RN
Iowa	B8MW36ZU56S
Kansas	TYPEVDEE24YT
Kentucky	LCD7WGS5X5
KGB Soldier	MNBVYRZP4QH
Louisiana	EHR5VVMHUSG
Maine	T5GYHQABGAC3
Maintenance Crew Member 1	T8EBSRK6F38
Maintenance Crew Member 2	YHQU74J6LLQ
Maintenance Crew Member 3	MFAJMUXZHHKJ
Male Scientist 1	ZFKHJKDEA2
Male Scientist 2	QQ4N3TPCL8PF
Male Scientist 3	CXFCF4FP9R6
Maryland	L2W9G5N76MH7
Massachusetts	ZLU2S3ULDEVF

SOLDIER	PASSWORD
Michigan	HGDRBUB5P3SA
Minnesota	EEBBM888ZRA
Mississippi	TBF7H9G6TJH7
Missouri	WJND6M9N738
Montana	9FYUFV29B2Y
Nebraska	MCNB5S5K47H
Nevada	Z9D4UGG8T4U6
New Hampshire	7NQYDQ9Y4KMP
New Jersey	LGHTBU9ZTGR
New Mexico	RGJCMHNLSX
New York	6PV39FKG6X
Normal Soldier Long Sleeve	QK3CMV373Y
Normal Soldier Long Sleeve Magazine Vest	D8RV32E9774
Normal Soldier Short Sleeve	N524ZHU9N4Z
Normal Soldier Short Sleeve Magazine Vest	6WXZA7PTT9Z
North Carolina	JGVT2XV47UZ
North Dakota	T5LSAVMPWZCY
Ocelot Female A	9FS7QYSHZ56N
Ocelot Female B	F94XDZSQSGJ8
Ocelot Female C	CRF8PZGXR28
Ocelot Unit	GE6MU3DXL3X
Ohio	AUWGAXWCA3D
Oklahoma	ZQT75NUJH8A3
Oregon	HKSD3PJ5E5
Pennsylvania	PL8GVVUM4HD
Pink Genome	7WRG3N2MRY2
Red Genome	9CM4SY23C7X8
Rhode Island	MMYC99T3QG
Seal	X56YCKZP2V
South Carolina	ZR4465MD8LK
South Dakota	RY3NUDDPMU3
Tengu Soldier	PHHB4TY4J2D
Tennessee	TD27326CX43U
Texas	QM84UPP6F3
Tsuhan soldier	A9KK7WYWVCV
USSR Female Soldier A	2VXUZQVH9R
USSR Female Soldier B	HPMRFSBXDJ3Y
USSR Female Soldier C	QXQVW9R3PZ
USSR Female Soldier D	GMC3M3LTPVW7
USSR Female Soldier E	5MXVX6UFPMZ5
USSR Female Soldier F	76AWS7WDAV
Utah	V7VRAYZ78GW
Vermont	L7T66LFZ63C8
Virginia	DRTCS77F5N
Washington	G3S4N42WWKTV
Washington DC	Y5YCFYHVZZW
West Virginia	72M8XR99B6

46

SOLDIER	PASSWORD	SOLDIER	PASSWORD
White Genome	QJ4ZTQSLUT8	Wyoming	C3THQ749RA
Wisconsin	K9BUN2BGLMT3	Yellow Genome	CE5HHYGTSSB

MLB 07: THE SHOW

SILVER ERA AND GOLD ERA TEAMS
At the Main menu, press Left, Up, Right, Down, Down, Left, Up, Down.

MAX BREAK PITCHES
Pause the game and press Right, Up, Right, Down, Up, Left, Left, Down.

MAX SPEED PITCHES
Pause the game and press Up, Left, Down, Up, Left, Right, Left, Down.

MLB 08: THE SHOW

CLASSIC FREE AGENTS AT THE PLAYER MOVEMENT MENU
At the main menu, press Left, Right, Up, Left, Right, Up, Right, Down.

SILVER ERA AND GOLDEN ERA TEAMS
At the main menu, press Right, Up, Right, Down, Down, Left, Up, Down.

BIG BALL
Pause the game and press Right, Down, Up, Left, Right, Left, Down, Up.

BIG HEAD MODE
Pause the game and press Right, Left, Down, Up, Left, Up, Down, Left.

SMALL HEAD MODE
Pause the game and press Left, Right, Down, Up, Right, Left, Down, Left.

N+

25 EXTRA LEVELS
At the main menu, hold L + R and press ✖, ◉, ✖, ◉, ✖, ✖, ◉.

NEED FOR SPEED CARBON: OWN THE CITY

UNLOCK EVERYTHING
At the start menu, press X, X, Right, Left, Square, Up, Down.

JET CAR
At the start menu, press Up, Down, Left, R1, L1, Circle, Triangle.

LAMBORGINI MERCIALAGO
At the start menu, press X, X, Up, Down, Left, Right, Circle, Circle.

TRANSFORMERS CAR
At the start menu, press X, X, X, Square, Triangle, Triangle, Up, Down.

NEOPETS PETPET ADVENTURE: THE WAND OF WISHING

START GAME WITH 5 CHOCOLATE TREATS

Enter treat4u as your Petpet's name. You can then rename name your character. The chocolate treats are shaped according to the character you chose.

POCKET POOL

ALL PICTURES AND VIDEOS

At the title screen, press L, R, L, L, R, R, L (x3), R (x3), L (x4), R (x4).

SEGA GENESIS COLLECTION

Before using the following cheats, select the ABC Control option. This sets the controller to the following: ⬤ is A, ✖ is B, ⬤ is C.

ALTERED BEAST

OPTIONS MENU

At the title screen, hold ✖ and press Start.

LEVEL SELECT

After enabling the Options menu, select a level from the menu. At the title screen, hold ⬤ and press Start.

BEAST SELECT

At the title screen, hold ⬤ + ✖ + ⬤ + Down/Left and then press Start

SOUND TEST

At the title screen, hold ⬤ + ⬤ + Up/Right and press Start.

COMIX ZONE

INVINCIBILITY

At the jukebox screen, press C on the following sounds:

3, 12, 17, 2, 2, 10, 2, 7, 7, 11

LEVEL SELECT

At the jukebox screen, press C on the following sounds:

14, 15, 18, 5, 13, 1, 3, 18, 15, 6

Press C on the desired level.

ECCO THE DOLPHIN

INVINCIBILITY

When the level name appears, hold ⬤ + Start until the level begins.

DEBUG MENU

Pause the game with Ecco facing the screen and press Right, ✖, ⬤, ✖, ⬤, Down, ⬤, Up.

INFINITE AIR

Enter LIFEFISH as a password

PASSWORDS

LEVEL	PASSWORD	LEVEL	PASSWORD
The Undercaves	WEFIDNMP	Deep City	DDXPQQLJ
The Vents	BQDPXJDS	City of Forever	MSDBRQLA
The Lagoon	JNSBRIKY	Jurassic Beach	IYCBUNLB
Ridge Water	NTSBZTKB	Pteranodon Pond	DMXEUNLI
Open Ocean	YWGTTJNI	Origin Beach	EGRIUNLB
Ice Zone	HZIFZBMF	Trilobite Circle	IELMUNLB
Hard Water	LRFJRQLI	Dark Water	RKEQUNLN
Cold Water	UYNFRQLC	City of Forever 2	HPQIGPLA
Island Zone	LYTIOQLZ	The Tube	JUMFKMLB
Deep Water	MNOPOQLR	The Machine	GXUBKMLF
The Marble	RJNTQQLZ	The Last Fight	TSONLMLU
The Library	RTGXQQLE		

FLICKY

ROUND SELECT

Begin a new game. Before the first round appears, hold ⬤ + ⬤ + Up + Start. Press Up or
Down to select a Round.

GAIN GROUND

LEVEL SELECT

At the Options screen, press ⬤, ⬤, ✖, ⬤.

GOLDEN AXE

LEVEL SELECT

Select Arcade Mode. At the character select, hold Down/Left +✖ and press Start. Press Up or
Down to select a level.

RISTAR

Select Passwords from the Options menu and enter the following:

LEVEL SELECT
ILOVEU

BOSS RUSH MODE
MUSEUM

TIME ATTACK MODE
DOFEEL

TOUGHER DIFFICULTY
SUPER

ONCHI MUSIC
MAGURO. Activate this from the Sound Test.

CLEARS PASSWORD
XXXXXX

GAME COPYRIGHT INFO
AGES

SONIC THE HEDGEHOG

LEVEL SELECT

At the title screen, press Up, Down, Left, Right. Hold ⬤ and press Start.

SONIC THE HEDGEHOG 2

LEVEL SELECT

Select Sound Test from the options. Press C on the following sounds in order: 19, 65, 09, 17.
At the title screen, hold ⬤ and press Start.

VECTORMAN

DEBUG MODE
At the options screen, press ⬤, ✖, ✖, ⬤, Down, ⬤, ✖, ✖, ⬤.

REFILL LIFE
Pause the game and press ⬤, ✖, Right, ⬤, ⬤, ⬤, Down, ⬤, ✖, Right, ⬤.

VECTORMAN 2

LEVEL SELECT
Pause the game and press Up, Right, ⬤,✖, ⬤, Down, Left, ⬤, Down.

EXTRA LIFE
Pause the game and press Right, Up, ✖, ⬤, Down, Up, ✖, Down, Up, ✖. Repeat for more lives.

FULL ENERGY
Pause the game and press ✖, ⬤, ✖, ⬤, Left, Up, Up.

NEW WEAPON
Pause the game and press ⬤, ⬤, Left, Left, Down, ⬤, Down. Repeat for more weapons.

SHREK THE THIRD

10,000 BONUS COINS
Press Up, Up, Down, Up, Right, Left at the Gift Shop.

THE SIMPSONS GAME

UNLIMITED POWER FOR ALL CHARACTERS
At the Extras menu, press ▲, Left, Right, ▲, ⬤, L.

ALL MOVIES
At the Extras menu, press ⬤, Left, ⬤, Right, ▲, R.

ALL CLICHÉS
At the Extras menu, press Left, ⬤, Right, ▲, Right, L.

THE SIMS 2: CASTAWAY

CHEAT GNOME
During a game, press L, R, Up, ✖, R. You can now use this Gnome to get the following during Live mode:

ALL PLANS
During a game, press ✖, R, ✖, R, ✖.

ALL CRAFT AND RESOURCES
During a game, press ⬤, ▲, R, Down, Down, Up.

MAX FOOD AND RESOURCES
During a game, press ⬤ (x4), L.

THE SIMS 2: PETS

CHEAT GNOME

During a game, press L, L, R, ✕, ✕, Up. Now you can enter the following cheats:

ADVANCE TIME 6 HOURS

During a game, press Up, Left, Down, Right, R.

GIVE SIM PET POINTS

During a game, press ▲, ●, ✕, ■, L, R.

$10,000

During a game, press ▲, Up, Left, Down, Right.

SPIDER-MAN: FRIEND OR FOE

NEW GOBLIN

At the stage complete screen, hold L + R and press ●, Down, ✕, Right, ■, Up, ▲, Left.

STAR WARS: THE FORCE UNLEASHED

CHEATS

Once you have accessed the Rogue Shadow, select Enter Code from the Extras menu. Now you can enter the following codes:

CHEAT	CODE
Invincibility	CORTOSIS
Unlimited Force	VERGENCE
1,000,000 Force Points	SPEEDER
All Force Powers	TYRANUS
Max Force Power Level	KATARN
Max Combo Level	COUNTDOOKU
Amplified Lightsaber Damage	LIGHTSABER

COSTUMES

Once you have accessed the Rogue Shadow, select Enter Code from the Extras menu. Now you can enter the following codes:

COSTUME	CODE	COSTUME	CODE
All Costumes	GRANDMOFF	Emperor Palpatine	PALPATINE
501st Legion	LEGION	General Rahm Kota	MANDALORE
Aayla Secura	AAYLA	Han Solo	NERFHERDER
Admiral Ackbar	ITSATWAP	Heavy trooper	SHOCKTROOP
Anakin Skywalker	CHOSENONE	Juno Eclipse	ECLIPSE
Asajj Ventress	ACOLYTE	Kento's Robe	WOOKIEE
Ceremonial Jedi Robes	DANTOOINE	Kleef	KLEEF
Chop'aa Notimo	NOTIMO	Lando Calrissian	SCOUNDREL
Classic stormtrooper	TK421	Luke Skywalker	T16WOMPRAT
Count Dooku	SERENNO	Luke Skywalker (Yavin)	YELLOWJCKT
Darth Desolous	PAUAN	Mace Windu	JEDIMASTER
Darth Maul	ZABRAK	Mara Jade	MARAJADE
Darth Phobos	HIDDENFEAR	Maris Brook	MARISBROOD
Darth Vader	SITHLORD	Navy commando	STORMTROOP
Drexl Roosh	DREXLROOSH	Obi Wan Kenobi	BENKENOBI

COSTUME	CODE	COSTUME	CODE
Proxy	HOLOGRAM	Sith Robes	HOLOCRON
Qui Gon Jinn	MAVERICK	Sith Stalker Armor	KORRIBAN
Shaak Ti	TOGRUTA	Twi'lek	SECURA
Shadow trooper	INTHEDARK		

STAR WARS: LETHAL ALLIANCE

ALL LEVELS
Select Create Profile from the Profiles menu and enter HANSOLO.

ALL LEVELS AND REFILL HEALTH WHEN DEPLETED
Select Create Profile from the Profiles menu and enter JD1MSTR.

REFILL HEALTH WHEN DEPLETED
Select Create Profile from the Profiles menu and enter B0BAF3T.

SUPER MONKEY BALL ADVENTURE

ALL CARDS
At the mode select, press ■, ▲, ●, ■, ▲, ●, ■, ▲, ●, ■, ▲, ●.

THRILLVILLE: OFF THE RAILS

$50,000
During a game, press ■, ●, ▲, ■, ●, ▲, ✕. Repeat this code as much as desired.

ALL PARKS
During a game, press ■, ●, ▲, ■, ●, ▲, ■.

ALL RIDES
During a game, press ■, ●, ▲, ■ ●, ▲, ▲. Some rides still need to be researched.

COMPLETE MISSIONS
During a game, press ■, ●, ▲, ■, ●, ▲, ●. Then, at the Missions menu, highlight a mission and press ● to complete that mission. Some missions have Bronze, Silver, and Gold objectives. For these missions the first press of ● earns the Bronze, the second earns the Silver, and the third earns the Gold.

TOMB RAIDER: LEGEND

You need to unlock the following cheats before they can be used.

BULLETPROOF
During a game, hold L and press ✕, R, ▲, R, ■, R.

DRAW ENEMY HEALTH
During a game, hold L and press ■, ●, ✕, R, R, ▲.

INFINITE ASSUALT RIFLE AMMO
During a game, hold L and press ✕, O, ✕, R, ■, ▲.

INFINITE GRENADE LAUNCHER
During a game, hold L and press R, ▲, R, ●, R, ■.

INFINITE SHOTGUN AMMO

During a game, hold L and press R, ●, ●, R, ●, ✕.

INFINITE SMG AMMO

During a game, hold L and press ●, ▲, R, R, ✕, ●.

ONE SHOT KILL

During a game, hold L and press ▲, ✕, ▲, ●, R, ●.

TEXTURELESS MODE

hold L and press R, ✕, ●, ✕, ▲, R.

WIELD EXCALIBUR

During a game, hold L and press ▲, ✕, ●, R, ▲, R.

WALL-E

KILL ALL

Select Cheats and then Secret Codes. Enter BOTOFWAR.

UNDETECTED BY ENEMIES

Select Cheats and then Secret Codes. Enter STEALTHARMOR.

LASERS CHANGE COLORS

Select Cheats and then Secret Codes. Enter RAINBOWLAZER.

CUBES ARE EXPLOSIVE

Select Cheats and then Secret Codes. Enter EXPLOSIVEWORLD.

LIGHTEN DARK AREAS

Select Cheats and then Secret Codes. Enter GLOWINTHEDARK.

GOGGLES

Select Cheats and then Secret Codes. Enter BOTOFMYSTERY.

GOLD TRACKS

Select Cheats and then Secret Codes. Enter GOLDENTRACKS.

WORLD CHAMPIONSHIP POKER 2: FEATURING HOWARD LEDERER

SKIP WEEK AND MONEY CHEATS

At the career world map, hold **R1**. Hold **L1** and release **R1**. Hold Up and release **L1**. Hold **L1** and release Up. Hold **R1** and release **L1**. While still holding **R1**, press Up/Down to skip weeks and Right/Left for money.

WRC: FIA WORLD RALLY CHAMPIONSHIP

UNLOCK EVERYTHING

Create a new profile with the name PADLOCK.

EXTRA AVATARS

Create a new profile with the name UGLYMUGS.

GHOST CAR

Create a new profile with the name SPOOKY.

SUPERCHARGER

Create a new profile with the name MAXPOWER.

TIME TRIAL GHOST CARS

Create a new profile with the name AITRIAL.

BIRD CAMERA

Create a new profile with the name dovecam.

REVERSES CONTROLS

Create a new profile with the name REVERSE.

X-MEN LEGENDS II: RISE OF APOCALYPSE

ALL CHARACTERS

At the Team Management screen, press Right, Left, Left, Right, Up, Up, Up, Start.

LEVEL 99 CHARACTERS

At the Team Management screen, press Up, Down, Up, Down, Left, Up, Left, Right, Start.

ALL SKILLS

At the Team Management screen, press Left, Right, Left, Right, Down, Up, Start.

SUPER SPEED

Pause the game and press Up, Up, Up, Down, Up, Down, Start.

UNLIMITED XTREME POWER

Pause the game and press Left, Down, Right, Down, Up, Up, Down, Up Start.

100,000 TECHBITS

At Forge or Beast's equipment screen, press Up, Up, Up, Down, Right, Right, Start.

ALL CINEMATICS

A the Review menu, press Left, Right, Right, Left, Down, Down, Left, Start.

ALL COMIC BOOKS

At the Review menu, press Right, Left, Left, Right, Up, Up, Right, Start.

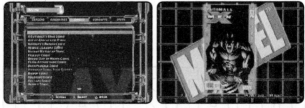

YU-GI-OH! GX TAG FORCE

BOOSTER PACK
At the card shop, press Up, Up, Down, Down, Left, Right, Left, Right, ✕, ◉.

YU-GI-OH! GX TAG FORCE 2

MIDDDAY CONSTELLATION BOOSTER PACK
When buying booster packs, press Up, Up, Down, Down, Left, Right, Left, Right, ✕, ◉.

YU-GI-OH! CARD PASSWORDS
Enter the following in the Password Machine to obtain for rental:

PASSWORD	EFFECT	PASSWORD	EFFECT
4-Starred Ladybug of Doom	83994646	After the Struggle	25345186
7 Colored Fish	23771716	Agido	16135253
A Cat of Ill Omen	24140059	Airknight Parshath	18036057
A Deal With Dark Ruler	06850209	Aitsu	48202661
A Feather of the Phoenix	49140998	Alkana Knight Joker	06150044
A Feint Plan	68170903	Alpha the Magnet Warrior	99785935
A Hero Emerges	21597117	Altar for Tribute	21070956
A Legendary Ocean	00295517	Amazon Archer	91869203
A Man With Wdjat	51351302	Amazoness Archers	67987611
A Rival Appears!	05728014	Amazoness Blowpiper	73574678
A Wingbeat of Giant Dragon	28596933	Amazoness Chain Master	29654737
A-Team: Trap Disposal Unit	13026402	Amazoness Paladin	47480070
Abare Ushioni	89718302	Amazoness Swords Woman	94004268
Absolute End	27744077	Amazoness Tiger	10979723
Absorbing Kid From the Sky	49771608	Ambulance Rescueroid	98927491
Abyss Soldier	18318842	Ambulanceroid	36378213
Abyssal Designator	89801755	Ameba	95174353
Acid Trap Hole	41356845	Amphibian Beast	67371383
Acrobat Monkey	47372349	Amphibious Bugroth MK-3	64342551
Adhesion Trap Hole	62325062	Amplifier	00303660
Adhesive Explosive	53828396	An Owl of Luck	23927567

PASSWORD	EFFECT	PASSWORD	EFFECT
Ancient Elf	93221206	Armed Dragon LV10	59464593
Ancient Gear	31557782	Armed Ninja	09076207
Ancient Gear Beast	10509340	Armed Samurai - Ben Kei	84430950
Ancient Gear Cannon	80045583	Armor Axe	07180418
Ancient Gear Castle	92001300	Armor Break	79649195
Ancient Gear Drill	67829249	Armored Lizard	15480588
Ancient Gear Golem	83104731	Armored Starfish	17535588
Ancient Gear Soldier	56094445	Armored Zombie	20277860
Ancient Lamp	54912977	Array of Revealing Light	69296555
Ancient Lizard Warrior	43230671	Arsenal Bug	42364374
Andro Sphinx	15013468	Arsenal Robber	55348096
Anteatereatingant	13250922	Arsenal Summoner	85489096
Anti-Aircraft Flower	65064143	Assault on GHQ	62633180
Anti-Spell	53112492	Astral Barrier	37053871
Apprentice Magician	09156135	Asura Priest	02134346
Appropriate	48539234	Aswan Apparition	88236094
Aqua Madoor	85639257	Atomic Firefly	87340664
Aqua Spirit	40916023	Attack and Receive	63689843
Arcane Archer of the Forest	55001420	Attack Reflector Unit	91989718
Archfiend of Gilfer	50287060	Aussa the Earth Charmer	37970940
Archfiend Soldier	49881766	Autonomous Action Unit	71453557
Archlord Zerato	18378582	Avatar of the Pot	99284890
Armaill	53153481	Axe Dragonute	84914462
Armed Changer	90374791	Axe of Despair	40619825
Armed Dragon LV 3	00980973	B. Skull Dragon	11901678
Armed Dragon LV 5	46384672	B.E.S. Covered Core	15317640
Armed Dragon LV 7	73879377	B.E.S. Crystal Core	22790789

PASSWORD	EFFECT	PASSWORD	EFFECT
B.E.S. Tetran	44954628	Berserk Dragon	85605684
Baby Dragon	88819587	Berserk Gorilla	39168895
Back to Square One	47453433	Beta the Magnet Warrior	39256679
Backfire	82705573	Bickuribox	25655502
Backup Soldier	36280194	Big Bang Shot	61127349
Bad Reaction to Simochi	40633297	Big Burn	95472621
Bait Doll	07165085	Big Core	14148099
Ballista of Rampart Smashing	00242146	Big Koala	42129512
Banisher of the Light	61528025	Big Shield Gardna	65240384
Bark of Dark Ruler	41925941	Big Wave Small Wave	51562916
Barrel Dragon	81480460	Big-Tusked Mammoth	59380081
Basic Insect	89091579	Bio-Mage	58696829
Battery Charger	61181383	Birdface	45547649
Batteryman AA	63142001	Black Illusion Ritual	41426869
Batteryman C	19733961	Black Luster Soldier - Envoy of the Beginning	72989439
Batteryman D	55401221	Black Pendant	65169794
Battle Footballer	48094997	Black Tyranno	38670435
Battle Ox	05053103	Blackland Fire Dragon	87564352
Battle-Scarred	94463200	Blade Knight	39507162
Bazoo The Soul-Eater	40133511	Blade Rabbit	58268433
Beast Soul Swap	35149085	Blade Skater	97023549
Beaver Warrior	32452818	Bladefly	28470714
Beckoning Light	16255442	Blast Held By a Tribute	89041555
Beelze Frog	49522489	Blast Magician	21051146
Begone, Knave	20374520	Blast with Chain	98239899
Behemoth the King of All Animals	22996376	Blasting the Ruins	21466326
Beiige, Vanguard of Dark World	33731070	Blazing Inpachi	05464695

PASSWORD	EFFECT	PASSWORD	EFFECT
Blind Destruction	32015116	Breaker the Magical Warrior	71413901
Blindly Loyal Goblin	35215622	Broww, Huntsman of Dark World	79126789
Block Attack	25880422	Brron, Mad King of Dark World	06214884
Blockman	48115277	Bubble Blaster	53586134
Blowback Dragon	25551951	Bubble Illusion	80075749
Blue-Eyes Shining Dragon	53347303	Bubble Shuffle	61968753
Blue-Eyes Toon Dragon	53183600	Bubonic Vermin	06104968
Blue-Eyes Ultimate Dragon	23995346	Burning Algae	41859700
Blue-Eyes White Dragon	89631139	Burning Beast	59364406
Blue-Winged Crown	41396436	Burning Land	24294108
Bokoichi the Freightening Car	08715625	Burst Breath	80163754
Bombardment Beetle	57409948	Burst Return	27191436
Bonding - H2O	45898858	Burst Stream of Destruction	17655904
Boneheimer	98456117	Buster Blader	78193831
Book of Life	02204140	Buster Rancher	84740193
Book of Moon	14087893	Butterfly Dagger - Elma	69243953
Book of Taiyou	38699854	Byser Shock	17597059
Boss Rush	66947414	Call of The Haunted	97077563
Bottom Dweller	81386177	Call of the Mummy	04861205
Bottomless Shifting Sand	76532077	Cannon Soldier	11384280
Bottomless Trap Hole	29401950	Cannonball Spear Shellfish	95614612
Bountiful Artemis	32296881	Card of Safe Return	57953380
Bowganian	52090844	Card Shuffle	12183332
Bracchio-Raidus	16507828	Castle of Dark Illusions	00062121
Brain Control	87910978	Cat's Ear Tribe	95841282
Brain Jacker	40267580	Catapult Turtle	95727991
Branch!	30548775	Cathedral of Nobles	29762407

PASSWORD	EFFECT	PASSWORD	EFFECT
Catnipped Kitty	96501677	Chorus of Sanctuary	81380218
Cave Dragon	93220472	Chthonian Alliance	46910446
Ceasefire	36468556	Chthonian Blast	18271561
Celtic Guardian	91152256	Chthonian Polymer	72287557
Cemetery Bomb	51394546	Chu-Ske the Mouse Fighter	08508055
Centrifugal	01801154	Clay Charge	22479888
Ceremonial Bell	20228463	Cliff the Trap Remover	06967870
Cetus of Dagala	28106077	Cobra Jar	86801871
Chain Burst	48276469	Cobraman Sakuzy	75109441
Chain Destruction	01248895	Cold Wave	60682203
Chain Disappearance	57139487	Collected Power	07565547
Chain Energy	79323590	Combination Attack	08964854
Chain Thrasher	88190453	Command Knight	10375182
Chainsaw Insect	77252217	Commander Covington	22666164
Change of Heart	04031928	Commencement Dance	43417563
Chaos Command Magician	72630549	Compulsory Evacuation Device	94192409
Chaos Emperor Dragon - Envoy of the End	82301904	Confiscation	17375316
Chaos End	61044390	Conscription	31000575
Chaos Greed	97439308	Continuous Destruction Punch	68057622
Chaos Necromancer	01434352	Contract With Exodia	33244944
Chaos Sorcerer	09596126	Contract With the Abyss	69035382
Chaosrider Gutaph	47829960	Contract with the Dark Master	96420087
Charcoal Inpachi	13179332	Convulsion of Nature	62966332
Charm of Shabti	50412166	Cost Down	23265313
Charubin the Fire Knight	37421579	Covering Fire	74458486
Chiron the Mage	16956455	Crab Turtle	91782219
Chopman the Desperate Outlaw	40884383	Crass Clown	93889755

PASSWORD	EFFECT
Creature Swap	31036355
Creeping Doom Manta	52571838
Crimson Ninja	14618326
Criosphinx	18654201
Cross Counter	37083210
Crush D. Gandra	64681432
Cure Mermaid	85802526
Curse of Aging	41398771
Curse of Anubis	66742250
Curse of Darkness	84970821
Curse of Dragon	28279543
Curse of the Masked Beast	94377247
Curse of Vampire	34294855
Cyber Dragon	70095154
Cyber End Dragon	01546123
Cyber Twin Dragon	74157028
Cyber-Dark Edge	77625948
Cyber-Stein	69015963
Cyberdark Dragon	40418351
Cyberdark Horn	41230939
Cyberdark Keel	03019642
D - Shield	62868900
D - Time	99075257
D. D. Assailant	70074904
D. D. Borderline	60912752
D. D. Crazy Beast	48148828
D. D. Dynamite	08628798

PASSWORD	EFFECT
D. D. M. - Different Dimension Master	82112775
D. D. Trainer	86498013
D. D. Trap Hole	05606466
D. D. Warrior Lady	07572887
Dancing Fairy	90925163
Dangerous Machine TYPE-6	76895648
Dark Artist	72520073
Dark Bat	67049542
Dark Blade	11321183
Dark Blade the Dragon Knight	86805855
Dark Driceratops	65287621
Dark Dust Spirit	89111398
Dark Elf	21417692
Dark Energy	04614116
Dark Factory of Mass Production	90928333
Dark Flare Knight	13722870
Dark Hole	53129443
Dark Magic Attack	02314238
Dark Magic Ritual	76792184
Dark Magician	46986414
Dark Magician Girl	38033121
Dark Magician of Chaos	40737112
Dark Magician's Tome of Black Magic	67227834
Dark Master - Zorc	97642679
Dark Mirror Force	20522190
Dark Paladin	98502113
Dark Room of Nightmare	85562745

PASSWORD	EFFECT	PASSWORD	EFFECT
Dark Sage	92377303	Destiny Hero - Captain Tenacious	77608643
Dark Snake Syndrome	47233801	Destiny Hero - Diamond Dude	13093792
Dark-Piercing Light	45895206	Destiny Hero - Doom Lord	41613948
Darkfire Dragon	17881964	Destiny Hero - Dreadmaster	40591390
Darkfire Soldier #1	05388481	Destiny Signal	35464895
Darkfire Soldier #2	78861134	Destroyer Golem	73481154
Darkworld Thorns	43500484	Destruction Ring	21219755
De-Spell	19159413	Dian Keto the Cure Master	84257639
Deal of Phantom	69122763	Dice Jar	03549275
Decayed Commander	10209545	Dimension Distortion	95194279
Dedication Through Light And Darkness	69542930	Dimensional Warrior	37043180
Deepsea Shark	28593363	Disappear	24623598
Dekoichi the Battlechanted Locomotive	87621407	Disarmament	20727787
Delinquent Duo	44763025	Disc Fighter	19612721
Demotion	72575145	Dissolverock	40826495
Des Counterblow	39131963	Divine Dragon Ragnarok	62113340
Des Croaking	44883830	Divine Wrath	49010598
Des Dendle	12965761	DNA Surgery	74701381
Des Feral Imp	81985784	DNA Transplant	56769674
Des Frog	84451804	Doitsu	57062206
Des Kangaroo	78613627	Dokurorider	99721536
Des Koala	69579761	Dokuroyaiba	30325729
Des Lacooda	02326738	Don Turtle	03493978
Des Wombat	09637706	Don Zaloog	76922029
Desert Sunlight	93747864	Doriado	84916669
Destertapir	13409151	Doriado's Blessing	23965037
Destiny Board	94212438	Dragon Seeker	28563545

PASSWORD	EFFECT
Dragon Treasure	01435851
Dragon Zombie	66672569
Dragon's Mirror	71490127
Dragon's Rage	54178050
Dragoness the Wicked Knight	70681994
Draining Shield	43250041
Dream Clown	13215230
Drillago	99050989
Drillroid	71218746
Dunames Dark Witch	12493482
Dust Tornado	60082867
Earth Chant	59820352
Earthbound Spirit	67105242
Earthquake	82828051
Eatgaboon	42578427
Ebon Magician Curran	46128076
Electro-Whip	37820550
Elegant Egotist	90219263
Element Dragon	30314994
Elemental Burst	61411502
Elemental Hero Avian	21844576
Elemental Hero Bladedge	59793705
Elemental Hero Bubbleman	79979666
Elemental Hero Burstinatrix	58932615
Elemental Hero Clayman	84327329
Elemental Hero Electrum/Erekshieler	29343734
Elemental Hero Flame Wingman	35809262

PASSWORD	EFFECT
Elemental Hero Mariner	14225239
Elemental Hero Necroid Shaman	81003500
Elemental Hero Neos	89943723
Elemental Hero Phoenix Enforcer	41436536
Elemental Hero Shining Flare Wingman	25366484
Elemental Hero Shining Phoenix Enforcer	88820235
Elemental Hero Sparkman	20721928
Elemental Hero Thunder Giant	61204971
Elemental Mistress Doriado	99414158
Elemental Recharge	36586443
Elf's Light	39897277
Emblem of Dragon Destroyer	06390406
Embodiment of Apophis	28649820
Emergency Provisions	53046408
Emes the Infinity	43580269
Empress Judge	15237615
Empress Mantis	58818411
Enchanted Javelin	96355986
Enchanting Mermaid	75376965
Enemy Controller	98045062
Enraged Battle Ox	76909279
Enraged Muka Muka	91862578
Eradicating Aerosol	94716515
Eternal Draught	56606928
Eternal Rest	95051344
Exhausting Spell	95451366
Exile of the Wicked	26725158

PASSWORD	EFFECT	PASSWORD	EFFECT
Exiled Force	74131780	Firewing Pegasus	27054370
Exodia Necross	12600382	Fireyarou	71407486
Exodia the Forbidden One	33396948	Fissure	66788016
Fairy Box	21598948	Five God Dragon (Five Headed Dragon)	99267150
Fairy Dragon	20315854	Flame Cerebrus	60862676
Fairy King Truesdale	45425051	Flame Champion	42599677
Fairy Meteor Crush	97687912	Flame Dancer	12883044
Faith Bird	75582395	Flame Ghost	58528964
Fatal Abacus	77910045	Flame Manipulator	34460851
Fenrir	00218704	Flame Swordsman	45231177
Feral Imp	41392891	Flame Viper	02830619
Fiber Jar	78706415	Flash Assailant	96890582
Fiend Comedian	81172176	Flower Wolf	95952802
Fiend Scorpion	26566878	Flying Fish	31987274
Fiend's Hand	52800428	Flying Kamakiri #1	84834865
Fiend's Mirror	31890399	Flying Kamakiri #2	03134241
Final Countdown	95308449	Follow Wind	98252586
Final Destiny	18591904	Foolish Burial	81439173
Final Flame	73134081	Forest	87430998
Final Ritual of the Ancients	60369732	Fortress Whale	62337487
Fire Darts	43061293	Fortress Whale's Oath	77454922
Fire Eye	88435542	Frenzied Panda	98818516
Fire Kraken	46534755	Frozen Soul	57069605
Fire Princess	64752646	Fruits of Kozaky's Studies	49998907
Fire Reaper	53581214	Fuh-Rin-Ka-Zan	01781310
Fire Sorcerer	27132350	Fuhma Shuriken	09373534
Firegrass	53293545	Fulfillment of the Contract	48206762

PASSWORD	EFFECT	PASSWORD	EFFECT
Fushi No Tori	38538445	Giant Germ	95178994
Fusion Gate	33550694	Giant Kozaky	58185394
Fusion Recovery	18511384	Giant Orc	73698349
Fusion Sage	26902560	Giant Rat	97017120
Fusion Weapon	27967615	Giant Red Seasnake	58831685
Fusionist	01641883	Giant Soldier of Stone	13039848
Gadget Soldier	86281779	Giant Trunade	42703248
Gagagigo	49003308	Gift of the Mystical Elf	98299011
Gaia Power	56594520	Giga Gagagigo	43793530
Gaia the Dragon Champion	66889139	Giga-Tech Wolf	08471389
Gaia the Fierce Knight	06368038	Gigantes	47606319
Gale Dogra	16229315	Gigobyte	53776525
Gale Lizard	77491079	Gil Garth	38445524
Gamble	37313786	Gilasaurus	45894482
Gamma the Magnet Warrior	11549357	Giltia the D. Knight	51828629
Garma Sword	90844184	Girochin Kuwagata	84620194
Garma Sword Oath	78577570	Goblin Attack Force	78658564
Garoozis	14977074	Goblin Calligrapher	12057781
Garuda the Wind Spirit	12800777	Goblin Elite Attack Force	85306040
Gatling Dragon	87751584	Goblin Thief	45311864
Gazelle the King of Mythical Beasts	05818798	Goblin's Secret Remedy	11868825
Gear Golem the Moving Fortress	30190809	Gogiga Gagagigo	39674352
Gearfried the Iron Knight	00423705	Golem Sentry	82323207
Gearfried the Swordmaster	57046845	Good Goblin Housekeeping	09744376
Gemini Elf	69140098	Gora Turtle	80233946
Getsu Fuhma	21887179	Graceful Charity	79571449
Giant Axe Mummy	78266168	Graceful Dice	74137509

PASSWORD	EFFECT	PASSWORD	EFFECT
Gradius	10992251	Guardian of the Labyrinth	89272878
Gradius' Option	14291024	Guardian of the Sea	85448931
Granadora	13944422	Guardian Sphinx	40659562
Grand Tiki Elder	13676474	Guardian Statue	75209824
Granmarg the Rock Monarch	60229110	Gust Fan	55321970
Gravedigger Ghoul	82542267	Gyaku-Gire Panda	09817927
Gravekeeper's Cannonholder	99877698	Gyroid	18325492
Gravekeeper's Curse	50712728	Hade-Hane	28357177
Gravekeeper's Guard	37101832	Hamburger Recipe	80811661
Gravekeeper's Servant	16762927	Hammer Shot	26412047
Gravekeeper's Spear Soldier	63695531	Hamon	32491822
Gravekeeper's Spy	24317029	Hand of Nephthys	98446407
Gravekeeper's Vassal	99690140	Hane-Hane	07089711
Graverobber's Retribution	33737664	Hannibal Necromancer	05640330
Gravity Bind	85742772	Hard Armor	20060230
Gray Wing	29618570	Harpie Girl	34100324
Great Angus	11813953	Harpie Lady 1	91932350
Great Long Nose	02356994	Harpie Lady 2	27927359
Great Mammoth of Goldfine	54622031	Harpie Lady 3	54415063
Green Gadget	41172955	Harpie Lady Sisters	12206212
Gren Maju Da Eiza	36584821	Harpie's Brother	30532390
Ground Attacker Bugroth	58314394	Harpies' Hunting Ground	75782277
Ground Collapse	90502999	Hayabusa Knight	21015833
Gruesome Goo	65623423	Headless Knight	05434080
Gryphon Wing	55608151	Heart of Clear Water	64801562
Gryphon's Feather Duster	34370473	Heart of the Underdog	35762283
Guardian Angel Joan	68007326	Heavy Mech Support Platform	23265594

PASSWORD	EFFECT	PASSWORD	EFFECT
Heavy Storm	19613556	Horus The Black Flame Dragon LV6	11224103
Helios - The Primordial Sun	54493213	Horus The Black Flame Dragon LV8	48229808
Helios Duo Megistus	80887952	Hoshiningen	67629977
Helios Tris Megiste	17286057	House of Adhesive Tape	15083728
Helping Robo for Combat	47025270	Howling Insect	93107608
Hero Barrier	44676200	Huge Revolution	65396880
HERO Flash!!	00191749	Human-Wave Tactics	30353551
Hero Heart	67951831	Humanoid Slime	46821314
Hero Kid	32679370	Humanoid Worm Drake	05600127
Hero Ring	26647858	Hungry Burger	30243636
Hero Signal	22020907	Hydrogeddon	22587018
Hidden Book of Spell	21840375	Hyena	22873798
Hidden Soldier	02047519	Hyozanryu	62397231
Hieracosphinx	82260502	Hyper Hammerhead	02671330
Hieroglyph Lithograph	10248192	Hysteric Fairy	21297224
High Tide Gyojin	54579801	Icarus Attack	53567095
Hiita the Fire Charmer	00759393	Illusionist Faceless Mage	28546905
Hino-Kagu-Tsuchi	75745607	Impenetrable Formation	96631852
Hinotama Soul	96851799	Imperial Order	61740673
Hiro's Shadow Scout	81863068	Inaba White Rabbit	77084837
Hitotsu-Me Giant	76184692	Incandescent Ordeal	33031674
Holy Knight Ishzark	57902462	Indomitable Fighter Lei Lei	84173492
Homunculus the Alchemic Being	40410110	Infernal Flame Emperor	19847532
Horn of Heaven	98069388	Infernal Queen Archfiend	08581705
Horn of Light	38552107	Inferno	74823665
Horn of the Unicorn	64047146	Inferno Fire Blast	52684508
Horus The Black Flame Dragon LV4	75830094	Inferno Hammer	17185260

PASSWORD	EFFECT	PASSWORD	EFFECT
Inferno Reckless Summon	12247206	Jar Robber	33784505
Inferno Tempest	14391920	Javelin Beetle	26932788
Infinite Cards	94163677	Javelin Beetle Pact	41182875
Infinite Dismissal	54109233	Jellyfish	14851496
Injection Fairy Lily	79575620	Jerry Beans Man	23635815
Inpachi	97923414	Jetroid	43697559
Insect Armor with Laser Cannon	03492538	Jinzo	77585513
Insect Barrier	23615409	Jinzo #7	32809211
Insect Imitation	96965364	Jirai Gumo	94773007
Insect Knight	35052053	Jowgen the Spiritualist	41855169
Insect Princess	37957847	Jowls of Dark Demise	05257687
Insect Queen	91512835	Judge Man	30113682
Insect Soldiers of the Sky	07019529	Judgment of Anubis	55256016
Inspection	16227556	Just Desserts	24068492
Interdimensional Matter Transporter	36261276	KA-2 Des Scissors	52768103
Invader From Another Dimension	28450915	Kabazauls	51934376
Invader of Darkness	56647086	Kagemusha of the Blue Flame	15401633
Invader of the Throne	03056267	Kaibaman	34627841
Invasion of Flames	26082229	Kaiser Dragon	94566432
Invigoration	98374133	Kaiser Glider	52824910
Iron Blacksmith Kotetsu	73431236	Kaiser Sea Horse	17444133
Island Turtle	04042268	Kaminari Attack	09653271
Jack's Knight	90876561	Kaminote Blow	97570038
Jade Insect Whistle	95214051	Kamionwizard	41544074
Jam Breeding Machine	21770260	Kangaroo Champ	95789089
Jam Defender	21558682	Karate Man	23289281
Jar of Greed	83968380	Karbonala Warrior	54541900

PASSWORD	EFFECT	PASSWORD	EFFECT
Karma Cut	71587526	Kycoo The Ghost Destroyer	88240808
Kelbek	54878498	La Jinn The Mystical Genie of The Lamp	97590747
Keldo	80441106	Labyrinth of Nightmare	66526672
Killer Needle	88979991	Labyrinth Tank	99551425
Kinetic Soldier	79853073	Lady Assailant of Flames	90147755
King Dragun	13756293	Lady Ninja Yae	82005435
King Fog	84686841	Lady of Faith	17358176
King of the Skull Servants	36021814	Larvas	94675535
King of the Swamp	79109599	Laser Cannon Armor	77007920
King of Yamimakai	69455834	Last Day of Witch	90330453
King Tiger Wanghu	83986578	Last Turn	28566710
King's Knight	64788463	Launcher Spider	87322377
Kiryu	84814897	Lava Battleguard	20394040
Kiseitai	04266839	Lava Golem	00102380
Kishido Spirit	60519422	Layard the Liberator	67468948
Knight's Title	87210505	Left Arm of the Forbidden One	07902349
Koitsu	69456283	Left Leg of the Forbidden One	44519536
Kojikocy	01184620	Legendary Black Belt	96438440
Kotodama	19406822	Legendary Flame Lord	60258960
Kozaky	99171160	Legendary Jujitsu Master	25773409
Kozaky's Self-Destruct Button	21908319	Legendary Sword	61854111
Kryuel	82642348	Leghul	12472242
Kumootoko	56283725	Lekunga	62543393
Kurama	85705804	Lesser Dragon	55444629
Kuriboh	40640057	Lesser Fiend	16475472
Kuwagata Alpha	60802233	Level Conversion Lab	84397023
Kwagar Hercules	95144193	Level Limit - Area A	54976796

PASSWORD	EFFECT	PASSWORD	EFFECT
Level Limit - Area B	03136426	Machine King	46700124
Level Modulation	61850482	Machine King Prototype	89222931
Level Up!	25290459	Machiners Defender	96384007
Levia-Dragon	37721209	Machiners Force	58054262
Light of Intervention	62867251	Machiners Sniper	23782705
Light of Judgment	44595286	Machiners Soldier	60999392
Lighten the Load	37231841	Mad Dog of Darkness	79182538
Lightforce Sword	49587034	Mad Lobster	97240270
Lightning Blade	55226821	Mad Sword Beast	79870141
Lightning Conger	27671321	Mage Power	83746708
Lightning Vortex	69162969	Magic Drain	59344077
Limiter Removal	23171610	Magic Jammer	77414722
Liquid Beast	93108297	Magical Cylinder	62279055
Little Chimera	68658728	Magical Dimension	28553439
Little-Winguard	90790253	Magical Explosion	32723153
Lizard Soldier	20831168	Magical Hats	81210420
Lord of D.	17985575	Magical Labyrinth	64389297
Lord of the Lamp	99510761	Magical Marionette	08034697
Lost Guardian	45871897	Magical Merchant	32362575
Luminous Soldier	57282479	Magical Plant Mandragola	07802006
Luminous Spark	81777047	Magical Scientist	34206604
Luster Dragon	11091375	Magical Thorn	53119267
Luster Dragon #2	17658803	Magician of Black Chaos	30208479
M-Warrior #1	56342351	Magician of Faith	31560081
M-Warrior #2	92731455	Magician's Circle	00050755
Machine Conversion Factory	25769732	Magician's Unite	36045450
Machine Duplication	63995093	Magician's Valkyrie	80304126

PASSWORD	EFFECT
Magnet Circle	94940436
Maha Vailo	93013676
Maharaghi	40695128
Maiden of the Aqua	17214465
Maji-Gire Panda	60102563
Maju Garzett	08794435
Makiu	27827272
Makyura the Destructor	21593977
Malevolent Nuzzler	99597615
Malfunction	06137095
Malice Ascendant	14255590
Malice Dispersion	13626450
Mammoth Graveyard	40374923
Man Eater	93553943
Man-Eater Bug	54652250
Man-Eating Black Shark	80727036
Man-Eating Treasure Chest	13723605
Man-Thro' Tro'	43714890
Manga Ryu-Ran	38369349
Manju of the Ten Thousand Hands	95492061
Manticore of Darkness	77121851
Marauding Captain	02460565
Marie the Fallen One	57579381
Marine Beast	29929832
Marshmallon	31305911
Marshmallon Glasses	66865880
Maryokutai	71466592

PASSWORD	EFFECT
Masaki the Legendary Swordsman	44287299
Mask of Brutality	82432018
Mask of Darkness	28933734
Mask of Restrict	29549364
Mask of Weakness	57882509
Masked Dragon	39191307
Masked of the Accursed	56948373
Masked Sorcerer	10189126
Mass Driver	34906152
Master Kyonshee	24530661
Master Monk	49814180
Master of Dragon Knight	62873545
Master of Oz	27134689
Mataza the Zapper	22609617
Mavelus	59036972
Maximum Six	30707994
Mazera DeVille	06133894
Mech Mole Zombie	63545455
Mecha-Dog Marron	94667532
Mechanical Hound	22512237
Mechanical Snail	34442949
Mechanical Spider	45688586
Mechanicalchaser	07359741
Meda Bat	76211194
Medusa Worm	02694423
Mefist the Infernal General	46820049
Mega Thunderball	21817254

PASSWORD	EFFECT	PASSWORD	EFFECT
Mega Ton Magical Cannon	32062913	Mind Control	37520316
Megamorph	22046459	Mind Haxorz	75392615
Megarock Dragon	71544954	Mind on Air	66690411
Melchid the Four-Face Beast	86569121	Mind Wipe	52718046
Memory Crusher	48700891	Mine Golem	76321376
Mermaid Knight	24435369	Minefield Eruption	85519211
Messenger of Peace	44656491	Minor Goblin Official	01918087
Metal Armored Bug	65957473	Miracle Dig	06343408
Metal Dragon	09293977	Miracle Fusion	45906428
Metallizing Parasite	07369217	Miracle Kid	55985014
Metalmorph	68540058	Miracle Restoring	68334074
Metalzoa	50705071	Mirage Dragon	15960641
Metamorphosis	46411259	Mirage Knight	49217579
Meteor B. Dragon	90660762	Mirage of Nightmare	41482598
Meteor Dragon	64271667	Mirror Force	44095762
Meteor of Destruction	33767325	Mirror Wall	22359980
Meteorain	64274292	Misfortune	01036974
Michizure	37580756	Mispolymerization	58392024
Micro-Ray	18190572	Mistobody	47529357
Mid Shield Gardna	75487237	Moai Interceptor Cannons	45159319
Mighty Guard	62327910	Mobius the Frost Monarch	04929256
Mikazukinoyaiba	38277918	Moisture Creature	75285069
Millennium Golem	47986555	Mokey Mokey	27288416
Millennium Scorpion	82482194	Mokey Mokey King	13803864
Millennium Shield	32012841	Mokey Mokey Smackdown	01965724
Milus Radiant	07489323	Molten Behemoth	17192817
Minar	32539892	Molten Destruction	19384334

PASSWORD	EFFECT	PASSWORD	EFFECT
Molten Zombie	04732017	Mystic Swordsman LV 6	60482781
Monk Fighter	03810071	Mystic Tomato	83011277
Monster Egg	36121917	Mystic Wok	80161395
Monster Eye	84133008	Mystical Beast Serket	89194033
Monster Gate	43040603	Mystical Elf	15025844
Monster Reborn	83764718	Mystical Knight of Jackal	98745000
Monster Recovery	93108433	Mystical Moon	36607978
Monster Reincarnation	74848038	Mystical Sand	32751480
Mooyan Curry	58074572	Mystical Sheep #2	30451366
Morale Boost	93671934	Mystical Shine Ball	39552864
Morphing Jar	33508719	Mystical Space Typhoon	05318639
Morphing Jar #2	79106360	Mystik Wok	80161395
Mother Grizzly	57839750	Mythical Beast Cerberus	55424270
Mountain	50913601	Nanobreaker	70948327
Mr. Volcano	31477025	Necklace of Command	48576971
Mudora	82108372	Necrovalley	47355498
Muka Muka	46657337	Needle Ball	94230224
Multiplication of Ants	22493811	Needle Burrower	98162242
Multiply	40703222	Needle Ceiling	38411870
Musician King	56907389	Needle Wall	38299233
Mustering of the Dark Scorpions	68191243	Needle Worm	81843628
Mysterious Puppeteer	54098121	Negate Attack	14315573
Mystic Horseman	68516705	Nemuriko	90963488
Mystic Lamp	98049915	Neo Aqua Madoor	49563947
Mystic Plasma Zone	18161786	Neo Bug	16587243
Mystic Swordsman LV 2	47507260	Neo the Magic Swordsman	50930991
Mystic Swordsman LV 4	74591968	Neo-Space	40215635

PASSWORD	EFFECT	PASSWORD	EFFECT
Neo-Spacian Aqua Dolphin	17955766	Obnoxious Celtic Guardian	52077741
Newdoria	04335645	Ocubeam	86088138
Next to be Lost	07076131	Offerings to the Doomed	19230407
Night Assailant	16226786	Ojama Black	79335209
Nightmare Horse	59290628	Ojama Delta Hurricane	08251996
Nightmare Penguin	81306586	Ojama Green	12482652
Nightmare Wheel	54704216	Ojama King	90140980
Nightmare's Steelcage	58775978	Ojama Trio	29843091
Nimble Momonga	22567609	Ojama Yellow	42941100
Nin-Ken Dog	11987744	Ojamagic	24643836
Ninja Grandmaster Sasuke	04041838	Ojamuscle	98259197
Ninjitsu Art of Decoy	89628781	Old Vindictive Magician	45141844
Ninjitsu Art of Transformation	70861343	Ominous Fortunetelling	56995655
Nitro Unit	23842445	Oni Tank T-34	66927994
Niwatori	07805359	Opti-Camaflauge Armor	44762290
Nobleman of Crossout	71044499	Opticlops	14531242
Nobleman of Extermination	17449108	Option Hunter	33248692
Nobleman-Eater Bug	65878864	Orca Mega-Fortress of Darkness	63120904
Non Aggression Area	76848240	Ordeal of a Traveler	39537362
Non-Fusion Area	27581098	Order to Charge	78986941
Non-Spellcasting Area	20065549	Order to Smash	39019325
Novox's Prayer	43694075	Otohime	39751093
Nubian Guard	51616747	Outstanding Dog Marron	11548522
Numinous Healer	02130625	Overdrive	02311603
Nutrient Z	29389368	Oxygeddon	58071123
Nuvia the Wicked	12953226	Painful Choice	74191942
0 - Oversoul	63703130	Paladin of White Dragon	73398797

PASSWORD	EFFECT	PASSWORD	EFFECT
Pale Beast	21263083	Piranha Army	50823978
Pandemonium	94585852	Pitch-Black Power Stone	34029630
Pandemonium Watchbear	75375465	Pitch-Black Warwolf	88975532
Parasite Paracide	27911549	Pitch-Dark Dragon	47415292
Parasitic Ticky	87978805	Poison Draw Frog	56840658
Patrician of Darkness	19153634	Poison Fangs	76539047
Patroid	71930383	Poison Mummy	43716289
Penguin Knight	36039163	Poison of the Old Man	08842266
Penumbral Soldier Lady	64751286	Polymerization	24094653
People Running About	12143771	Possessed Dark Soul	52860176
Perfect Machine King	18891691	Pot of Avarice	67169062
Performance of Sword	04849037	Pot of Generosity	70278545
Petit Angel	38142739	Pot of Greed	55144522
Petit Dragon	75356564	Power Bond	37630732
Petit Moth	58192742	Power Capsule	54289683
Phantasmal Martyrs	93224848	Precious Card from Beyond	68304813
Phantom Beast Cross-Wing	71181155	Premature Burial	70828912
Phantom Beast Thunder-Pegasus	34961968	Prepare to Strike Back	04483989
Phantom Beast Wild-Horn	07576264	Prevent Rat	00549481
Pharaoh's Servant	52550973	Prickle Fairy	91559748
Pharonic Protector	89959682	Primal Seed	23701465
Phoenix Wing Wind Blast	63356631	Princess Curran	02316186
Photon Generator Unit	66607691	Princess of Tsurugi	51371017
Pikeru's Circle of Enchantment	74270067	Princess Pikeru	75917088
Pikeru's Second Sight	58015506	Protective Soul Ailin	11678191
Pinch Hopper	26185991	Protector of the Sanctuary	24221739
Pineapple Blast	90669991	Protector of the Throne	10071456

PASSWORD	EFFECT	PASSWORD	EFFECT
Proto-Cyber Dragon	26439287	Reborn Zombie	23421244
Pumpking the King of Ghosts	29155212	Reckless Greed	37576645
Punished Eagle	74703140	Recycle	96316857
Pyramid of Light	53569894	Red Archery Girl	65570596
Pyramid Turtle	77044671	Red Gadget	86445415
Queen's Knight	25652259	Red Medicine	38199696
Rabid Horseman	94905343	Red Moon Baby	56387350
Rafflesia Seduction	31440542	Red-Eyes B. Chick	36262024
Raging Flame Sprite	90810762	Red-Eyes B. Dragon	74677422
Raigeki	12580477	Red-Eyes Black Metal Dragon	64335804
Raigeki Break	04178474	Red-Eyes Darkness Dragon	96561011
Rain Of Mercy	66719324	Reflect Bounder	02851070
Rainbow Flower	21347810	Regenerating Mummy	70821187
Rallis the Star Bird	41382147	Reinforcement of the Army	32807846
Rancer Dragonute	11125718	Release Restraint	75417459
Rapid-Fire Magician	06337436	Relinquished	64631466
Rare Metalmorph	12503902	Reload	22589918
Raregold Armor	07625614	Remove Trap	51482758
Raviel, Lord of Phantasms	69890967	Rescue Cat	14878871
Ray & Temperature	85309439	Rescueroid	24311595
Ray of Hope	82529174	Reshef the Dark Being	62420419
Re-Fusion	74694807	Respect Play	08951260
Ready For Intercepting	31785398	Return from the Different Dimension	27174286
Really Eternal Rest	28121403	Return of the Doomed	19827717
Reaper of the Cards	33066139	Reversal of Graves	17484499
Reaper of the Nightmare	85684223	Reversal Quiz	05990062
Reasoning	58577036	Revival Jam	31709826

PASSWORD	EFFECT	PASSWORD	EFFECT
Right Arm of the Forbidden One	70903634	Royal Keeper	16509093
Right Leg of the Forbidden One	08124921	Royal Knight	68280530
Ring of Defense	58641905	Royal Magical Library	70791313
Ring of Destruction	83555666	Royal Surrender	56058888
Ring of Magnetism	20436034	Royal Tribute	72405967
Riryoku Field	70344351	Ruin, Queen of Oblivion	46427957
Rising Air Current	45778932	Rush Recklessly	70046172
Rising Energy	78211862	Ryu Kokki	57281778
Rite of Spirit	30450531	Ryu Senshi	49868263
Ritual Weapon	54351224	Ryu-Kishin Clown	42647539
Robbin' Goblin	88279736	Ryu-Kishin Powered	24611934
Robbin' Zombie	83258273	Saber Beetle	49645921
Robolady	92421852	Sacred Crane	30914564
Robotic Knight	44203504	Sacred Phoenix of Nephthys	61441708
Roboyarou	38916461	Saggi the Dark Clown	66602787
Rock Bombardment	20781762	Sakuretsu Armor	56120475
Rock Ogre Grotto	68846917	Salamandra	32268901
Rocket Jumper	53890795	Salvage	96947648
Rocket Warrior	30860696	Samsara	44182827
Rod of the Mind's Eye	94793422	Sand Gambler	50593156
Roll Out!	91597389	Sand Moth	73648243
Root Water	39004808	Sangan	26202165
Rope of Life	93382620	Sanwitch	53539634
Rope of Spirit	37383714	Sasuke Samurai	16222645
Roulette Barrel	46303688	Sasuke Samurai #2	11760174
Royal Command	33950246	Sasuke Samurai #3	77379481
Royal Decree	51452091	Sasuke Samurai #4	64538655

PASSWORD	EFFECT	PASSWORD	EFFECT
Satellite Cannon	50400231	Shifting Shadows	59237154
Scapegoat	73915051	Shinato's Ark	60365591
Scarr, Scout of Dark World	05498296	Shinato, King of a Higher Plane	86327225
Science Soldier	67532912	Shining Abyss	87303357
Scroll of Bewitchment	10352095	Shining Angel	95956346
Scyscraper	63035430	Shooting Star Bow - Ceal	95638658
Sea Serpent Warrior of Darkness	42071342	Silent Insect	40867519
Sealmaster Meisei	02468169	Silent Magician Lv4	73665146
Second Coin Toss	36562627	Silent Magician Lv8	72443568
Second Goblin	19086954	Silent Swordsman LV3	01995985
Secret Barrel	27053506	Silent Swordsman LV5	74388798
Self-Destruct Button	57585212	Silent Swordsman LV7	37267041
Senri Eye	60391791	Sillva, Warlord of Dark World	32619583
Serial Spell	49398568	Silpheed	73001017
Serpent Night Dragon	66516792	Silver Fang	90357090
Serpentine Princess	71829750	Simorgh, Bird of Divinity	14989021
Servant of Catabolism	02792265	Simultaneous Loss	92219931
Seven Tools of the Bandit	03819470	Sinister Serpent	08131171
Shadow Ghoul	30778711	Sixth Sense	03280747
Shadow Of Eyes	58621589	Skill Drain	82732705
Shadow Tamer	37620434	Skilled Dark Magician	73752131
Shadowknight Archfiend	09603356	Skilled White Magician	46363422
Shadowslayer	20939559	Skull Archfiend of Lightning	61370518
Share the Pain	56830749	Skull Descovery Knight	78700060
Shield & Sword	52097679	Skull Dog Marron	86652646
Shield Crash	30683373	Skull Invitation	98139712
Shien's Spy	07672244	Skull Lair	06733059
Shift	59560625	Skull Mariner	05265750

PASSWORD	EFFECT	PASSWORD	EFFECT
Skull Red Bird	10202894	Souleater	31242786
Skull Servant	32274490	Souls Of The Forgotten	04920010
Skull Zoma	79852326	Space Mambo	36119641
Skull-Mark Ladybug	64306248	Spark Blaster	97362768
Skyscraper	63035430	Sparks	76103675
Slate Warrior	78636495	Spatial Collapse	20644748
Smashing Ground	97169186	Spear Cretin	58551308
Smoke Grenade of the Thief	63789924	Spear Dragon	31553716
Snatch Steal	45986603	Spell Canceller	84636823
Sogen	86318356	Spell Economics	04259068
Soitsu	60246171	Spell Purification	01669772
Solar Flare Dragon	45985838	Spell Reproduction	29228529
Solar Ray	44472639	Spell Shield Type-8	38275183
Solemn Judgment	41420027	Spell Vanishing	29735721
Solemn Wishes	35346968	Spell-Stopping Statute	10069180
Solomon's Lawbook	23471572	Spellbinding Circle	18807108
Sonic Duck	84696266	Spherous Lady	52121290
Sonic Jammer	84550200	Sphinx Teleia	51402177
Sorcerer of Dark Magic	88619463	Spiral Spear Strike	49328340
Soul Absorption	68073522	Spirit Barrier	53239672
Soul Exchange	68005187	Spirit Caller	48659020
Soul of Purity and Light	77527210	Spirit Message A	94772232
Soul Release	05758500	Spirit Message I	31893528
Soul Resurrection	92924317	Spirit Message L	30170981
Soul Reversal	78864369	Spirit Message N	67287533
Soul Tiger	15734813	Spirit of Flames	13522325
Soul-Absorbing Bone Tower	63012333	Spirit of the Breeze	53530069

PASSWORD	EFFECT	PASSWORD	EFFECT
Spirit of the Harp	80770678	Success Probability 0%	06859683
Spirit of the Pharaoh	25343280	Summon Priest	00423585
Spirit Reaper	23205979	Summoned Skull	70781052
Spirit Ryu	67957315	Summoner of Illusions	14644902
Spiritual Earth Art - Kurogane	70156997	Super Conductor Tyranno	85520851
Spiritual Energy Settle Machine	99173029	Super Rejuvenation	27770341
Spiritual Fire Art - Kurenai	42945701	Super Robolady	75923050
Spiritual Water Art - Aoi	06540606	Super Roboyarou	01412158
Spiritual Wind Art - Miyabi	79333300	Supply	44072894
Spiritualism	15866454	Susa Soldier	40473581
St. Joan	21175632	Swarm of Locusts	41872150
Stamping Destruction	81385346	Swarm of Scarabs	15383415
Star Boy	08201910	Swift Gaia the Fierce Knight	16589042
Statue of the Wicked	65810489	Sword Hunter	51345461
Staunch Defender	92854392	Sword of Deep-Seated	98495314
Stealth Bird	03510565	Sword of Dragon's Soul	61405855
Steam Gyroid	05368615	Sword of the Soul Eater	05371656
Steamroid	44729197	Swords of Concealing Light	12923641
Steel Ogre Grotto #1	29172562	Swords of Revealing Light	72302403
Steel Ogre Grotto #2	90908427	Swordsman of Landstar	03573512
Stim-Pack	83225447	Symbol of Heritage	45305419
Stop Defense	63102017	System Down	18895832
Storming Wynn	29013526	T.A.D.P.O.L.E.	10456559
Stray Lambs	60764581	Tactical Espionage Expert	89698120
Strike Ninja	41006930	Tailor of the Fickle	43641473
Stronghold	13955608	Taunt	90740329
Stumbling	34646691	Tenkabito Shien	41589166

PASSWORD	EFFECT	PASSWORD	EFFECT
Terra the Terrible	63308047	The Forceful Sentry	42829885
Terraforming	73628505	The Forces of Darkness	29826127
Terrorking Archfiend	35975813	The Forgiving Maiden	84080938
Terrorking Salmon	78060096	The Furious Sea King	18710707
Teva	16469012	The Graveyard in the Fourth Dimension	88089103
The Agent of Creation - Venus	64734921	The Gross Ghost of Fled Dreams	68049471
The Agent of Force - Mars	91123920	The Hunter With 7 Weapons	01525329
The Agent of Judgment - Saturn	91345518	The Illusionary Gentleman	83764996
The Agent of Wisdom - Mercury	38730226	The Immortal of Thunder	84926738
The All-Seeing White Tiger	32269855	The Kick Man	90407382
The Big March of Animals	01689516	The Last Warrior From Another Planet	86099788
The Bistro Butcher	71107816	The Law of the Normal	66926224
The Cheerful Coffin	41142615	The League of Uniform Nomenclature	55008284
The Creator	61505339	The Legendary Fisherman	03643300
The Creator Incarnate	97093037	The Light - Hex Sealed Fusion	15717011
The Dark - Hex Sealed Fusion	52101615	The Little Swordsman of Aile	25109950
The Dark Door	30606547	The Masked Beast	49064413
The Dragon Dwelling in the Cave	93346024	The Portrait's Secret	32541773
The Dragon's Bead	92408984	The Regulation of Tribe	00296499
The Earl of Demise	66989694	The Reliable Guardian	16430187
The Earth - Hex Sealed Fusion	88696724	The Rock Spirit	76305638
The Emperor's Holiday	68400115	The Sanctuary in the Sky	56433456
The End of Anubis	65403020	The Second Sarcophagus	04081094
The Eye Of Truth	34694160	The Secret of the Bandit	99351431
The Fiend Megacyber	66362965	The Shallow Grave	43434803
The Flute of Summoning Dragon	43973174	The Spell Absorbing Life	99517131
The Flute of Summoning Kuriboh	20065322		

PASSWORD	EFFECT	PASSWORD	EFFECT
The Thing in the Crater	78243409	Tongyo	69572024
The Third Sarcophagus	78697395	Toon Cannon Soldier	79875176
The Trojan Horse	38479725	Toon Dark Magician Girl	90960358
The Unhappy Girl	27618634	Toon Defense	43509019
The Unhappy Maiden	51275027	Toon Gemini Elf	42386471
The Warrior Returning Alive	95281259	Toon Goblin Attack Force	15270885
Theban Nightmare	51838385	Toon Masked Sorcerer	16392422
Theinen the Great Sphinx	87997872	Toon Mermaid	65458948
Thestalos the Firestorm Monarch	26205777	Toon Summoned Skull	91842653
Thousand Dragon	41462083	Toon Table of Contents	89997728
Thousand Energy	05703682	Toon World	15259703
Thousand Needles	33977496	Tornado Bird	71283180
Thousand-Eyes Idol	27125110	Tornado Wall	18605135
Thousand-Eyes Restrict	63519819	Torpedo Fish	90337190
Threatening Roar	36361633	Torrential Tribute	53582587
Three-Headed Geedo	78423643	Total Defense Shogun	75372290
Throwstone Unit	76075810	Tower of Babel	94256039
Thunder Crash	69196160	Tradgedy	35686187
Thunder Dragon	31786629	Transcendent Wings	25573054
Thunder Nyan Nyan	70797118	Trap Dustshoot	64697231
Thunder of Ruler	91781589	Trap Hole	04206964
Time Seal	35316708	Trap Jammer	19252988
Time Wizard	71625222	Treeborn Frog	12538374
Timeater	44913552	Tremendous Fire	46918794
Timidity	40350910	Tri-Horned Dragon	39111158
Token Festevil	83675475	Triage	30888983
Token Thanksgiving	57182235	Trial of Nightmare	77827521

PASSWORD	EFFECT	PASSWORD	EFFECT
Trial of the Princesses	72709014	Ultimate Insect LV3	34088136
Triangle Ecstasy Spark	12181376	Ultimate Insect LV5	34830502
Triangle Power	32298781	Ultimate Insect LV7	19877898
Tribe-Infecting Virus	33184167	Ultimate Obedient Fiend	32240937
Tribute Doll	02903036	Ultimate Tyranno	15894048
Tribute to The Doomed	79759861	Ultra Evolution Pill	22431243
Tripwire Beast	45042329	Umi	22702055
Troop Dragon	55013285	Umiiruka	82999629
Tsukuyomi	34853266	Union Attack	60399954
Turtle Oath	76806714	United Resistance	85936485
Turtle Tiger	37313348	United We Stand	56747793
Twin Swords of Flashing Light	21900719	Unity	14731897
Twin-Headed Beast	82035781	Unshaven Angler	92084010
Twin-Headed Behemoth	43586926	Upstart Goblin	70368879
Twin-Headed Fire Dragon	78984772	Uraby	01784619
Twin-Headed Thunder Dragon	54752875	Uria, Lord of Sealing Flames	06007213
Twin-Headed Wolf	88132637	V-Tiger Jet	51638941
Two Thousand Needles	83228073	Valkyrion the Magna Warrior	75347539
Two-Man Cell Battle	25578802	Vampire Genesis	22056710
Two-Mouth Darkruler	57305373	Vampire Lord	53839837
Two-Pronged Attack	83887306	Vampire Orchis	46571052
Tyhone	72842870	Vengeful Bog Spirit	95220856
Type Zero Magic Crusher	21237481	Victory D	44910027
Tyranno Infinity	83235263	Vilepawn Archfiend	73219648
Tyrant Dragon	94568601	VW-Tiger Catapult	58859575
UFOroid	07602840	VWXYZ-Dragon Catapult Cannon	84243274
UFOroid Fighter	32752319	W-Wing Catapult	96300057
Ultimate Insect LV1	49441499	Waboku	12607053

PASSWORD	EFFECT	PASSWORD	EFFECT
Wall of Revealing Light	17078030	Wolf Axwielder	56369281
Wandering Mummy	42994702	Woodborg Inpachi	35322812
Warrior Dai Grepher	75953262	Woodland Sprite	06979239
Warrior of Zera	66073051	Worm Drake	73216412
Wasteland	23424603	Wroughtweiler	06480253
Water Dragon	85066822	Wynn the Wind Charmer	37744402
Water Omotics	02483611	X-Head Cannon	62651957
Wave Motion Cannon	38992735	Xing Zhen Hu	76515293
Weed Out	28604635	XY-Dragon Cannon	02111707
Whiptail Crow	91996584	XYZ-Dragon Cannon	91998119
Whirlwind Prodigy	15090429	XZ-Tank Cannon	99724761
White Dragon Ritual	09786492	Y-Dragon Head	65622692
White Horn Dragon	73891874	Yamata Dragon	76862289
White Magical Hat	15150365	Yami	59197169
White Magician Pikeru	81383947	Yata-Garasu	03078576
White Ninja	01571945	Yellow Gadget	13839120
Wicked-Breaking Flameberge-Baou	68427465	Yellow Luster Shield	04542651
Wild Nature's Release	61166988	Yomi Ship	51534754
Winged Dragon, Guardian of the Fortress #1	87796900	YZ-Tank Dragon	25119460
Winged Kuriboh	57116033	Z-Metal Tank	64500000
Winged Kuriboh LV10	98585345	Zaborg the Thunder Monarch	51945556
Winged Minion	89258225	Zero Gravity	83133491
Winged Sage Falcos	87523462	Zoa	24311372
Wingweaver	31447217	Zolga	16268841
Witch Doctor of Chaos	75946257	Zombie Tiger	47693640
Witch of the Black Forest	78010363	Zombyra the Dark	88472456
Witch's Apprentice	80741828	Zure, Knight of Dark World	07459013
Witty Phantom	36304921		

GAME BOY® ADVANCE

TABLE OF CONTENTS

BANJO PILOT

GRUNTY

Defeat Grunty in the Broomstick battle race. Then, you can purchase Grunty from Cheato.

HUMBA WUMBA

Defeat Humba Wumba in the Jiggu battle race. Then, you can purchase Humba Wumba from Cheato.

JOLLY

Defeat Jolly in the Pumpkin battle race. Then, you can purchase Jolly from Cheato.

KLUNGO

Defeat Klungo in the Skull battle race. Then, you can purchase Klungo from Cheato.

BARBIE AS THE PRINCESS AND THE PAUPER

PASSWORDS

LEVEL	PASSWORD
1-2	Preminger, Wolfie, Erika, Serafina
1-3	Wolfie, Preminger, Serafina, Preminger
1-4	Preminger, Wolfie, Serfania, Wolfie
Boss 1	Serafina, Woflia. Erika, Preminger
2-1	Princess Anneliese, Preminger, Wolfie, Erika
2-2	Preminger, Princess Anneliese, Wolfie, Erika
2-3	Preminger, Serafina, Preminger, Erika
2-4	Serafina, Erika, Preminger, Wolfie
Boss 2	Preminger, Erika, Serafina, Wolfie

LEVEL	PASSWORD
3-1	Wolfie, Preminger, Wolfie, Erika
3-2	Serafina, Preminger, Erika, Serafina
3-3	Erika, Wolfie, Serafina, Princess Anneliese
3-4	Erika, Serafina, Erika, Preminger
Boss 3	Preminger, Serafina, Princess Anneliese, Serafina
4-1	Wolfie, Serafina, Preminger, Serafina
4-2	Preminger, Serafina, Princess Anneliese, Preminger
4-3	Wolfie, Serafina, Erika, Serafina
Boss 4	Erika, Serafina, Princess Anneliese, Wolfie
Final Boss	Erika, Princess Anneliese, Princess Anneliese, Man
Arcade Level	Princess Anneliese, Serafina, Erika, Wolfie

CASTLEVANIA: ARIA OF SORROW

NO ITEMS

Start a new game with the name NOUSE to use no items in the game.

NO SOULS

Start a new game with the name NOSOUL to use no souls in the game.

DK: KING OF SWING

ATTACK BATTLE 3

At the Title screen, press Up + L + A + B to bring up a password screen. Enter 65942922.

CLIMBING RACE 5

At the Title screen, press Up + L + A + B to bring up a password screen. Enter 55860327.

OBSTACLE RACE 4

At the Title screen, press Up + L + A + B to bring up a password screen. Enter 35805225.

UNLOCK TIME ATTACK

Complete the game as DK.

UNLOCK DIDDY MODE

Collect 24 medals as DK.

UNLOCK BUBBLES

Complete Diddy Mode with 24 Medals.

UNLOCK KREMLING

Collect 6 gold medals in Jungle Jam.

UNLOCK KING K. ROOL

Collect 12 gold medals in Jungle Jam.

DONKEY KONG COUNTRY 2: DIDDY KONG'S QUEST

ALL LEVELS

Select Cheats from the Options and enter freedom.

START WITH 15 LIVES

Select Cheats from the Options and enter helpme.

START WITH 55 LIVES

Select Cheats from the Options and enter weakling.

START WITH 10 BANANA COINS

Select Cheats from the Options and enter richman.

START WITH 50 BANANA COINS

Select Cheats from the Options and enter wellrich.

NO DK OR HALF WAY BARRELS

Select Cheats from the Options and enter rockard.

MUSIC PLAYER

Select Cheats from the Options and enter onetime.

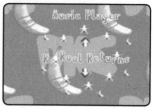

CREDITS

Select Cheats from the Options and enter kredits.

FINAL FANTASY I & II: DAWN OF SOULS

FF I TILE GAME

During a game of Final Fantasy I and after you get the ship, hold A and press B about 55 times.

FF II CONCENTRATION GAME

Once you obtain the Snowcraft, hold B and press A about 20 times.

MONSTER FORCE

RESTART LEVEL

Pause the game, hold L + R and press A.

FINISH LEVEL

During a game, hold L + R + A and press Up.

PLAY AS MINA OR DREW

At the Character Select screen, hold L + R + B and press Right.

RATATOUILLE

INVINCIBILITY

Enter X4V!3RJ as a password.

ALL CHAPTERS

Enter H3L!X3! as a password. Press L or R at the Chapter Select screen.

ALL MINI-GAMES

Enter JV4ND1Z as a password.

ALL BONUS PICTURES

Enter 3R1CQRR as a password.

RIVER CITY RANSOM EX

Select the status menu and change your name to the following:

MAX STATS
DAMAX

$999999.99
PLAYA

CUSTOM CHAR
XTRA0

CUSTOM SELF
XTRA1

CUSTOM MOVE
XTRA2

CLEAR SAVE
ERAZE

TECHNIQUES 1
FUZZY. This group includes Mach Punch, Dragon Kick, Acro Circus, Grand Slam, Javelin Man, Slick Trick, Nitro Port, Twin Kick, Deadly Shot, Top Spin, Helicopter, Torpedo.

TECHNIQUES 2
WUZZY. This group includes Slap Happy, Pulper, Headbutt, Kickstand, Big Bang, Wheel Throw, Glide Chop, Head Bomb, Chain Chump, Jet Kick, Shuriken, Flip Throw.

TECHNIQUES 3
WAZZA. This group includes Boomerang, Charge It, Bat Fang, Flying Kick, Speed Drop, Bomb Blow, Killer Kick, Bike Kick, Slam Punk, Dragon Knee, God Fist, Hyperguard.

TECHNIQUES 4
BEAR*. This group includes PhoenixWing, Inlines, Springlines, Rocketeers, Air Merc's Narcishoes, Magic Pants, Pandora Box, Skaterz, Custom Fit.

STREET FIGHTER ALPHA 3

ALL FIGHTERS
At the Title screen, press Left, Right, Down, Right, L, L, A, L, L, B, R, A, Up.

ALL MODES
At the Title screen, press A, Up, A, L, R, Right, L, Right, A, Down, Right. Now press L, Right, A, R, Up,L, Right, B, A, Up, Right, Down, Right.

PLAY AS SUPER BISON
At the Character Select screen, hold Start and select Bison.

PLAY AS SHIN AKUMA
At the Character Select screen, hold Start and select Akuma.

ALTERNATE COSTUMES
At the Character Select screen, press L or R.

FINAL BATTLE
At the Speed Select option, hold A + B.

THAT'S SO RAVEN 2: SUPERNATURAL STYLE

COSTUME MODE
At the Title screen, press Left, Right, Up, Down, B, B, B, Up, Down.

UNLIMITED ENERGY MODE
At the Title screen, press B, B, L, R, Up, Down, Up, Left, Right.

TRON 2.0: KILLER APP

ALL MINIGAMES

At the Title screen, press Left, Left, Left, Left, Up, Right, Down, Down, Select.

YOSHI TOPSY-TURVY

CHALLENGE MODE AND CHALLENGE 1

Defeat Bowser for the second time in Story Mode.

CHALLENGES 2, 3, 4

Complete the Egg Gallery in Story Mode.

FINAL CHALLENGE

Earn all Golds in Story Mode.

YU-GI-OH! 7 TRIALS TO GLORY: WORLD CHAMPIONSHIP TOURNAMENT 2005

PURPLE TITLE SCREEN

Completing the game changes the Title screen from blue to purple. To switch it back, press Up, Up, Down, Down, Left, Right, Left, Right, B, A at the Title screen.

CREDITS

Defeat the game, then press Up, Up, Down, Down, Left, Right, Left, Right, B, A.

CARD PASSWORDS

At the password machine, press R and enter a password.

Refer to the Card List for YU-GI-OH! GX TAG FORCE for PSP. All cards are not available in World Championship Tournament 2005.

YU-GI-OH! ULTIMATE MASTERS: WORLD CHAMPIONSHIP TOURNAMENT 2006

CARD PASSWORDS

Enter the 8-digit codes at the Password screen to unlock that card for purchase.

Refer to the Card List for YU-GI-OH! GX TAG FORCE for PSP. All cards may not be available in World Championship Tournament 2006.

ONLINE GAMING FOR KIDS: A PARENT'S GUIDE

There are plenty of great games for kids on the web, but which ones are best for your child, and how can you ensure they don't visit a site that's inappropriate? Well, we've compiled a list of the most impressive and trusted gaming spots for kids, then categorized them by age. Visit these sites and determine which ones your family likes most. Once you've determined your favorites, you can then make accessing them safe and easy for your child in just three easy steps:

SAFE ONLINE GAMING FOR KIDS IS AS EASY AS 1-2-3

Here's how you can create an **Internet Games Page**—a clickable document that allows your child to safely and easily visit your family's favorite online gaming sites for kids:

1. Open a new document in Microsoft Word.

2. Type in the URLs (web site addresses) listed in this section that best suit your child's age and interests. After each URL, press ENTER to automatically create a Hyperlink. The address will then appear in blue, underlined text. That means you can now immediately go directly to that web site. Just simultaneously press CTRL and click on the blue text. See our note below for an even slicker way of doing this.

3. When your list of Hyperlinks is complete, save the file as "[Your Child's Name]'s Games" on your computer's desktop.

USER FRIENDLY LINKS

If you think your child might find it difficult to visit his or her favorite gaming sites by selecting from a list of long and sometimes unwieldy internet addresses, then customize the lists on your Internet Games Page by renaming them with something more easily recognizable. It's easy. Simply type the name you wish to use (LEGO, for example) and highlight the word with your mouse. Next, right-click on the highlighted word and select Hyperlink from the window that pops up. Another window appears with your cursor blinking in the empty Address field. Type in the proper URL here (in the case of LEGO, you would type *http://play.lego.com/en-US/games/default.aspx* into this field), then click OK. The word you highlighted on your Internet Games Page is now a Hyperlink. Using our example, that means your child can simply click on (left-click + CTRL) the word "LEGO" to visit the LEGO games site!

You can even dress up this document with colorful backgrounds and clip art to make it even more personal and appealing. You now have a resource that provides a quick and easy path for your child to access safe and entertaining gaming sites that you have seen and trust.

BEST ONLINE GAMING SITES FOR KIDS

AGES 6-7

Children in this age group may not be as computer savvy and certainly won't have as strong reading skills as older kids. So, you may need to get your child started until he or she is comfortable navigating these sites and properly understands the rules to the games.

Slime Slinger Online Game

http://www.scholastic.com/goosebumps/slimeslinger/game.asp

A fun game based on the popular Goosebumps series of books.

Highlights Kids Hidden Pictures

http://www.highlightskids.com/GamesandGiggles/HiddenPics/HIddenPixFlashObjects/h8hpiArchive.asp

More than just games, these puzzle-oriented offerings really work kids' brains.

CBeebies at BBC

http://www.bbc.co.uk/cbeebies/fun/

Lots of cute games for younger kids.

Yahooligans Games

http://kids.yahoo.com/games

Loads of fun for all ages here with a wide variety of games—puzzles, arcade, sports, and more!

Pauly's Playhouse Online Games

http://www.paulysplayhouse.com/paulys_playhouse/game_page/game.html

Wow! This site has loads of games! All pretty simple and most will have your child smiling from ear to ear.

Nick.com Games Online

http://www.nick.com/games/

Lots of good stuff here, all associated with Nick programming your child likely already enjoys.

Lego Club Games

http://play.lego.com/en-US/games/default.aspx

Great interactive fun that provides exciting scenarios that simulate playing with LEGO toys.

Barbie.com Games Online

http://barbie.everythinggirl.com/activities/fun_games/

Let's face it, most girls like Barbie as much as just about anything. The games your daughter plays on this site will not disappoint her.

EDUCATIONAL FUN!

Chicken Stacker
http://pbskids.org/lions/games/stacker.html

You can never go wrong with PBS when it comes to kids, and Between the Lions is one of many great programs. This game based on the show helps kids build their word power.

Play Kids Games.com
http://www.playkidsgames.com/

Everything from simple math to word and memory games. Plenty here for the next age group, too.

AGES 8-9

Scholastic Games
http://www.scholastic.com/kids/games.htm

Solve mysteries, answer trivia, collect rare items, and more! The fun here is all based on popular books with this age group.

Monkeybar TV
http://www.hasbro.com/monkeybartv/default.cfm?page=Entertainment/OnlineGames/GameHome

This site is operated by Hasbro, so the characters and toys associated with the games are all classics known and loved by kids and adults—including Transformers, Littlest Pet Shop, Monopoly, GI Joe, Star Wars, and others!

Cartoon Network Games Online
http://www.cartoonnetwork.com/games/index.html

Kids can't read and be active all the time, and cartoons nicely fill that need to laugh and take it easy. This is the place for hilarious games from hilarious toons.

I Spy Games Online
http://www.scholastic.com/ispy/play/

Another Scholastic gem that allows kids to use their powers of observation online!

Disney Channel Games Online
http://tv.disney.go.com/disneychannel/games/index.html

Have you ever met a fourth grader who isn't into Disney? Hannah Montana, Kim Possible, Zack & Cody… what's not to like? This site has plenty of familiar faces and fun stuff.

Kidnetics Active Online Games
http://www.kidnetic.com/

Fitness focused games and projects for kids.

EDUCATIONAL FUN!

Multiplication.com
http://www.multiplication.com/interactive_games.htm

Cute and entertaining games that help make multiplication tables a breeze.

Big Brainz
http://www.bigbrainz.com/index.php

Download a free version of Timez Attack, a great looking action video game that boosts multiplication skills!

AGE 10 & UP

If you're 10 years old, there's no reason you still can't have fun playing the games we've listed in the previous two age groups, but these will definitely appeal to the big kids.

ESPN Arcade
http://arcade.espn.go.com/

ESPN offers a great online gaming site for kids who are into sports.

Zeeks Board & Card Games
http://games.zeeks.com/games.php

Tons of free games. Not just entertaining, but a little edgy, too!

Battleship
http://www.creativecalendar.com/kids/Games/games_battleship.html

Everyone loves this game. Just as much fun online!

OTHER ONLINE GAMES

We've put these games in a separate category because they're not free. They either require a subscription or the purchase of a toy to play. However, you may consider these investments worthwhile, as they do provide some intriguing gameplay and learning opportunities. Plus, if your kids are into gaming or have friends who are, they're bound to mention these sites to you sooner or later, so you may want to see what they're all about for yourself.

Webkinz
http://www.webkinz.com/

Requires you to buy a toy before "adopting" one online, but the game experience is pretty cool. Webkinz allows kids to care for their pet, including improving and furnishing its home. Earn Kinz cash by answering trivia and doing other fun activities.

Club Penguin
http://www.clubpenguin.com/

This subscription-based online game is operated by Disney. It provides a kid-friendly virtual world where children can play games, have fun, and interact with each other...but it's not free.